Nigel Foster's

SURF KAYAKING

"A great tutorial for all those who wish to learn more about the growing sport of paddle-powered surfing."
—Dick Wold, Senior Editor of *Paddler* magazine's "Surf Zone"

Help Us Keep This Guide Up to Date

Every effort has been made by the author and editors to make this guide as accurate and useful as possible. However, many things can change after a guide is published—new products and information become available, regulations change, techniques evolve, etc.

We would love to hear from you concerning your experiences with this guide and how you feel it could be improved and be kept up to date. While we may not be able to respond to all comments and suggestions, we'll take them to heart and we'll also make certain to share them with the author. Please send your comments and suggestions to the following address:

The Globe Pequot Press
Reader Response/Editorial Department
P.O. Box 833
Old Saybrook, CT 06475

Or you may e-mail us at:

editorial@globe-pequot.com

Thanks for your input, and happy travels!

Nigel Foster's
SURF KAYAKING

Nigel Foster

The
Globe
Pequot
Press

Old Saybrook, Connecticut

Cover design by Adam Schwartzman
Page design by Deborah V. Nicolais

Photo Credits
Unless noted otherwise, all photos on each page are by the named photographer.
Cover photos by Terry Harlow
Photos by Karin Mentzing: page 6 (top).
Photos by Kristin Nelson: pages 1; 2; 8 (bottom); 17 (top); 19 (top); 20; 21; 22; 37; 38; 39; 40; 41; 42; 43; 44; 45; 46; 47; 48; 51; 52; 53; 54; 56; 57; 58 (bottom); 60 (bottom and top); 63 (right top, center, and bottom) 65; 66; 67 (bottom right); 69; 70; 71; 72; 73; 75 (all but left photo on page); 76; 78; 79; 80; 81; 84; and 87.
Photos by Nigel Foster: pages 3; 4; 5; 6 (bottom left, center, and right); 7; 8 (top); 10; 16; 17 (center and bottom); 23; 24; 27; 28; 29; 33; 34; 35; 36; 58 (top); 63 (left top, center, and bottom); 64 (top), 67 (bottom left); and 86 .
Photo by Peter Foster: page 75 (left).
Photos by Terry Harlow: pages 19 (bottom); 60 (center); 61; 64 (bottom); 67 (top); and 87.

Library of Congress Cataloging-in-Publication Data

Foster, Nigel.
    [Surf kayaking]
    Nigel Foster's surf kayaking / Nigel Foster. — 1st ed.
      p.   cm.
    Includes index.
    ISBN 0–7627–0218–4
    1. Sea kayaking.   2. Ocean waves.   I. Title.
  GV788.5.F77   1998
  797.1'224—dc21

98–24363
CIP

First Edition / First Printing
PRINTED IN CANADA

To my daughter Kate,
that in sharing her love of the water she might know her father better

ACKNOWLEDGMENTS

Thanks to the many people who helped in the creation of this book, including the following:

David Egan
Joey Yeaple
Rich McBride of Salamander
Alistair Wilson of Lendal, U.K.
Scott Williams of Sweetwater Kayaks
North Cove Outfitters, Connecticut
Pacific Watersports, Washington
Michael Powers
Terry Harlow
Peter Foster
Karin Mentzing

Especially, thanks to Kristin Nelson for her tireless assistance, support, and encouragement throughout the project.

CONTENTS

Introduction

Riding on a mercurial evening sea.

As a teenager I was totally hooked on kayak surfing. The school I attended offered ice skating as a winter sports alternative to the more standard soccer. The teacher in charge of this activity seldom checked to see whether we students had skipped off. He would always check who was going to the ice and make his list, offering a warning that he'd come down later to make sure we were all there. Two of us avid kayakers used to have a difficult time walking the seafront from the bus stop to the ice rink, and if the weather was good for surfing we would pick our own alternative sport, justifying it to each other with the reassurance that we were not actually skipping sports but simply attending a different one.

One particularly good day the sea was wild and we enjoyed long rides close to the Palace Pier. But this was the day the warning that our teacher would check on us was not idle. He stood on the seafront watching—but not recognizing—us surfing for some time, thinking how dangerous it looked, before continuing to the ice rink. It was there, finding us missing from the party, that he was told we were surfing instead. From then on I was grounded, playing soccer each week.

But I've remained an avid kayaker nonetheless.

Combining many technical skills and an excellent workout, surf kayaking is an exhilarating paddle sport, with a style of movement that can be as individual to you as any performing art. I relish every sensation—from apprehension as I survey the beach and check out the waves, to the first push forward from the beach onto the water to paddle out, to that moment when I paddle to catch a ride and my hull takes off down that steep wall of water. Then I'm in a different world. To skim along the face of a steep wave controlling a small craft with the ease and grace of a gliding bird amid what appears to be outrageously violent conditions is a joy to experience. Every movement seems slowed and heightened as I maneuver to keep on that steepest part of the wave, responding to the changing conditions yet carving my own signature across the water. The sequences of movements both challenge and please me.

Though by the end of a session I am weary, the impression of the sequences that truly worked for me that day glow in my memory like the aftertaste of a good red wine or a quality chocolate. Overlaid are images of my surroundings: visions of glowing green waves, of white spray in the air, the hiss of the water spitting bubbles, the rifle crack of a hollow wave breaking, and the cries of sheer high spirits from my companions. But above all I'm left with a priceless sense of inner calmness and the happy knowledge that despite countless rides in the surf, no two have ever been the same.

1 Equipment

Because of differing sea conditions and different body shapes and weights, no single set of equipment can suit everyone. Equipment is a matter of personal choice. Try out whatever you can in your search for what suits you best.

Different Kayaks for Different Conditions

People surf in all kinds of kayaks in all kinds of waves. Part of the joy of surfing is that it can be pleasurable in such a variety of craft. If you don't have a specially designed surf kayak, that shouldn't

A 1970s beach scene in Cornwall, England, including a trailer laden with a variety of slalom and surf kayaks.

prevent you from having fun surfing. In this section I describe different types of kayaks and how they function as surfing craft. In the end you should match your choice of craft to the conditions you most often surf. If you generally surf on windblown storm surf, then a short, narrow, sharp-railed wave ski will not allow you as much fun as a longer, less sharply railed surf kayak or a slalom kayak. In general sharper rails are best on cleaner waves, more rounded rails are more forgiving on ragged waves, and longer craft are easier to manage on less steep waves and on larger waves.

Whatever kayak design you choose, you should check a few things before you go into the surf. Check your deck and hull for signs of wear and for leaks. The seat should be fastened securely. To prevent sliding back in your seat in the event of a reverse ender, you need some form of support for your lower back, such as a backstrap.

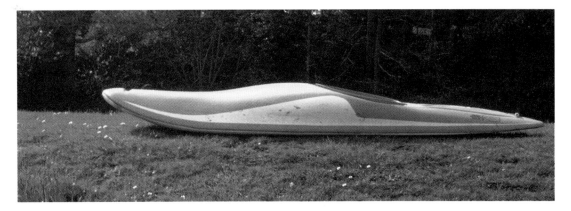

A surf kayak. Note the small stern.

A footbrace system is essential. Ideally this should be a complete bulkhead, preventing your feet from going past. (Adjustable pedal-type footbraces are not as safe. In the event of an ender, when the kayak hits the sand, your feet may slip off. If you have this kind of footbrace, fill the end of the kayak with minicell foam to prevent your feet from slipping off.) The kayak's stern should be completely filled with airbags for flotation in case of a wet exit. A waterlogged boat with maximum flotation is much easier to get to shore than one with minimal flotation. Having flotation in both ends of the kayak is essential.

At each end should be an *end grab:* something secure for you to hold onto in the event of a swim, for a swimmer to hold onto if you need to help a swimmer to shore, and for you to grab your kayak during awkward landings. Make certain you cannot trap your fingers in your end grab even if the kayak is rolled in the surf. Check end grabs regularly for wear and replace them when necessary; the strain when they are used in surf is considerable.

Surf Kayaks

Surf kayaks were developed in the 1970s specifically for riding waves. Imagine the bottom of a surfboard with a deck and seat fitted and you have a surf kayak. Surf kayaks have planing hulls with the seat set close to the stern to minimize pearling. Typically they have a little rocker, particularly in the bow, but the section from the seat aft can be completely flat or rockered. For holding an edge on a diagonal run, there must be a *rail*—that is, an edge between the flatness of the

The hull of a surf kayak resembles a surf board.

hull and the side. This is normally more rounded near the bow, to provide a forgiving surface when the bow catches the water, and sharper toward the middle and the stern, to make it easier to hold an edge. You will notice this increased grip especially when you edge the kayak into the face of a wave on a diagonal run. Sharper edges can be more difficult to handle than softer, more rounded edges in turbulent water. Sharp edges are best suited to quality surf, whereas a softer rail might be more appropriate if you regularly ride storm surf.

The shape of the stern determines how much control you have. Fine control is typically more difficult with a round, flat stern and more precise with a pintail, although a short, narrow stern can present stability problems when you are sitting still.

A white-water kayak. Alongside, the two airbags that fill the stern.

Whitewater Kayaks

In recent years whitewater kayaks have become increasingly appropriate for wave riding, as paddlers are seeking to progress by attempting more skilled moves on moderate water rather than by attempting to descend more extreme rivers. Length has decreased to 6 to 9 feet, making for maneuverable craft with hull shapes suitable for spinning yet with sufficient rail to hold an edge well. There are still, however, many longer craft in the 13-foot range that respond well on a wave. Many slalom shapes work in surf because of the low volume in the stern, which allows the stern to sit in the wave, and their sharp rails edge well. The extra length of these craft make catching a wave easier, for they have the speed to catch less steep waves and also faster waves. Longer hulls are generally less easily maneuvered but can be graceful on carved turns and fast on diagonal runs. If the hull profile is fairly flat, you may be able to perform 360s on the face of wave, but these are difficult with this length of kayak. Cutback turns on steep waves need to be more quickly performed than in shorter craft, to prevent the nose from burying and because of the greater hull speed.

If your Kayak has pointed ends, then pad the ends in ethafoam or some other tough cushioning material and tape the pads securely in place. There have been some horrific accidents in surf when the sharp bows of slalom kayaks have impaled other water users.

Sea Kayaks

Sea kayaks pass regularly through surf zones on their way to cruise the coast. Inevitably through their use in coastal environments, they are often used for surfing, although that is rarely their design function. I prefer a V-shaped stern running from a chine rather than a rounded stern section. The chine provides an edge that can be used similarly to the way a rail is used. A rounded hull near the stern provides a somewhat unstable shape for planing.

Wave Skis

In the 1970s and 1980s, wave skis seemed a logical progression from surf kayaks. They are lightweight when crafted similarly to the way a

Sea kayaks heading out through the surf.

surfboard is—that is, shaped from a blank of foam and coated in a skin of fiberglass. A ski is easy to climb back onto from the water, and it has no cockpit to become waterlogged; although this means you need not be able to roll to surf one, it is possible to roll a wave ski, provided it is fitted with foot straps and a lap strap. General performance is related to shape and weight, with lighter, livelier handling in the short skis. Longer skis are better in larger waves.

Although I love the performance of a lightweight wave ski, I still prefer the lower-body protection offered by a closed-cockpit surf kayak. This is protection from the physical impact of breaking waves, as well as warmth offered by the enclosed space. Wave skis are best suited to warm-water environments, but, of course, the same could be said for board surfing—you just need to be well clad!

Before you surf a wave ski, familiarize yourself with how to release your feet from the foot loops and how to release the lap strap. The lap strap should have a quick-release mechanism. Practice the procedure upright until it is automatic, then capsize and repeat the sequence underwater.

In addition to the straps that hold you in your seat, on a wave ski you should wear an ankle leash. This is a line that will prevent your ski from escaping should you release from it. A runaway ski floats perfectly and will be carried inshore by waves as a danger to others using the water, leaving you at best with a long swim. A safety leash will ensure that your ski remains with you, where you can remount it and continue to surf.

A wave ski. Compare the profile with that of the surf kayak.

The wave ski is fitted with a lap strap and a foot strap. Here, the ankle leash is hooked around the lap strap.

Skegs prevent the tail from skidding. The steps in the hull here also help.

The short paddle is typical for surfing.

Paddles

A short paddle is ideal for wave skis and surf kayaks. I am six feet tall and use a paddle length of 200 centimeters in surf as compared with a length between 108 and 116 centimeters for sea kayaking. You can get good acceleration using a short paddle, and there is less leverage on the blade when you are underwater trying to hold it or bring it into position for a roll. Rapid ruddering changes also become easier with a short paddle in the tight space beside a steep wave.

Though many surfers use an asymmetrical blade or a symmetrical blade that is rounded off at the corners, I think this is a matter of personal preference rather than function. In general symmetrical blades on the market are more likely to be built for the rigors of whitewater rather than touring, whereas asymmetrical blades are frequently more lightly constructed. Nevertheless, you will find a curved blade more effective than a flat one. The concave curve of the power face gives you better acceleration by holding water more effectively, while the convex curve of the back of the blade makes it plane smoothly in the low-brace position. Choose a paddle shaft with a degree of spring in it; otherwise your hands and elbows may suffer from the jarring effect. The difference is particularly noticeable in surf.

Some surfers like to use a paddle leash to attach the paddle to their wrist. This is not something I do myself, but I have no strong feelings against using these leashes.

Personal Flotation Device (PFD) or Buoyancy Aid

This is an essential part of your equipment, offering extra flotation whenever you swim. In the event of a long swim to shore after a wet exit, a PFD can be a great help. It will also keep you on the surface if an injury occurs. Always check that you have fastened and adjusted your PFD according to the manufacturer's instructions.

Look for flotation of around 50 to 60 newtons. Your PFD should fit snugly without impairing your ability to breathe, and it should be worn so that it cannot ride up around your face when you swim. I look for freedom of arm movement through the normal range of paddle strokes. The cut around the armholes needs to be generous. Because you should always wear this garment on the water, comfort is paramount.

Helmet

Although you may think of a helmet in terms of whitewater paddling, where the greatest risk is hitting rocks on the bottom, in surf kayaking you are far more likely to suffer a blow from your own paddle in the turbulence of a broken wave, or from your deck as you tuck in a roll position to wait for a wave to pass. In my experience both situations occur frequently enough to justify wear-

A helmet is essential, preferably in a bright color. This one has ear protection and a simple faceguard. The anorak here has a latex neck seal.

ing a helmet. A helmet will also protect you from inadvertent impact with the beach in shallow water. (You might also consider a simple faceguard to extend the protection to your nose.)

Look for a snug fit, with cushioned protection. Ideally your helmet should cover your whole forehead and remain in position even when you try to pull it upward. Though ear covering can help protect your ears, beware of helmets with vents at the ear but with internal padding surrounding the earwell as a foam lining. A complete surrounding can lead to ear damage when water claps against the hole and forces air or water under pressure into the only available place, your ear. Make sure there is a larger and easier way for air and water to escape from behind such a vent than into your ear.

I used to think that holes in a kayaking helmet were essential to permit water to drain out. In fact water drains out from the open end of the helmet, not through the holes. But there are two useful reasons for having holes in your helmet.

This white helmet shows poorly in surf.

The first is for ventilation—a vented helmet is cooler than an unvented one. The second is to let you know when it's windy—when the wind speed reaches about 40 to 50 miles per hour, it will whistle across the holes. Whether or not to choose a helmet with holes is a matter of personal preference.

An uncovered head is a major source of heat loss; keeping your head warm will help you think better. Thus in cold water wear a thin neoprene hood under your helmet for added insulation.

Ear Protection

Repeated ingress of cold water can cause a bony growth in the ear canal. Called osteoma, the condition can in time grow to block the canal, causing deafness. Surfers know this condition as *surfer's ear*, although it is known by other names in other watersports. Wearing specially fitted earplugs is a sensible precaution to prevent water being forced in.

Clothing

Immersion or repeated rolls, as well as paddling out through the soup, will chill you rapidly if you are not adequately dressed. Your clothing should both insulate and protect you from windchill.

What you choose to wear will depend on the temperature of both the air and the water. A neoprene "Farmer John" is a popular choice, the neoprene providing insulation and a degree of padding for the knees inside the kayak. Combine this with underlayers of fleece (thin layers of wool have better insulating properties in the water but are less available than fleece) to cover your arms and torso, and a long-sleeved anorak over the top. The snugger your outer garments fit, the less water resistance you'll experience when paddling out through the soup. But most important are (1) protection from cold and windchill and (2) freedom of movement. Don't expect to feel as free as a bird in a heavy gladiator suit.

A waterproof jacket with latex wrist and neck seals is close to ideal as an outer-shell garment, but the neck seal will almost certainly give you that "lynched" look by rubbing into your neck until it is raw. Causing this is primarily the salt in the water, combined with the constant head turning to watch waves. Wear a thin scarf or a turtleneck beneath your anorak and pull the fabric up between your neck and the neck seal for a good compromise. I opt for a more comfortable but less watertight seal and resign myself to getting a little wetter inside.

A complete drysuit is another outer-shell alternative, with fleece layers underneath—but again beware of the neck seal.

Stretching Your Neck (Seal)

Neck seals on new garments can be restrictive to the point of giving you that "lynched" look. Rather than trimming the opening to make it wider, stretch it over a bowl 5 inches greater in circumference than the seal hole and leave it overnight. Stretching the latex will make it fit looser without damaging the integrity of the seal edge. Little nicks in the rubber at the edge caused by trimming will frequently provide a tearing point when you stretch the seal over your head.

*When wearing a latex neck seal on the beach during breaks or while keeping watch, you can wear around your neck a thin plastic tubular ring known as a **diver's ring**. Lift the neck seal over the ring to hold it away from your neck until you next go afloat. The neck ring will relieve the pressure from your neck and allow some ventilation of your drysuit.*

Shoes

Feet have a hard time. When your kayak is tossed around in the surf, your feet will almost certainly find any uncomfortable edges of any internal footbrace structures, and any sand will end up abrading your heels. I like to wear a small, lightweight beach shoe with a tough sole. Neoprene boots are notorious for their particular aroma, but they work well to keep your feet warm in cold water. Avoid barefeet. From my observation surf paddlers seem to get more cuts on their feet than on any other body part. I used to before I began wearing shoes.

Sprayskirt

A neoprene sprayskirt is almost an essential. Nylon ones tend to collapse in the soup. Before buying one check the depth of the groove around the cockpit rim. Polyethylene kayaks often have a coaming too shallow to permit the rectangular section rubber strip on some sprayskirts to hold effectively, and even give a poor purchase for some of the thick elastic used on other sprayskirts. Your sprayskirt must withstand the considerable weight of water when a wave breaks onto it. The body tube should fit snugly over the clothing you most often wear for surfing, with little free space for water to trickle down. The sprayskirt should also have a release tab to help you release the deck quickly. Check your sprayskirt for holes and ensure that the release strap is secure. The waistband must fit snugly around your waist or you will get a lot of water in your kayak.

Footpump

A pump such as the specially designed "Lendal" footpump fits onto the footbrace of a kayak. Pumping with one or both feet expels water from the kayak through an outlet in the deck—a great alternative to going ashore to drain your kayak.

A Lendal footpump—excellent for keeping your kayak dry.

Color and Visibility in Surf

From the viewpoint of safety, it's a good idea to be seen easily in surf. Although the color of your kayak will help, often only your head, shoulders, and paddle blade are visible. Consider a brightly colored helmet that will contrast with the water, a colorful PFD, and brightly hued paddle blades. Dark colors show up poorly, as does white.

Distress Signals You Can Carry

Your most readily available distress signal is your paddle. Hold it in the air and wave it from side to side, making sure that the face of the blade, rather than its edge, is toward the people from whom you are trying to attract attention. Additional distress signals, such as pyrotechnic flares, marine VHF radios, and cell phones require sturdy and reliable waterproof wrapping before they can be carried dry in such a harsh, watery environment. Carry distress signals on your person rather than in your kayak. Your worst-case scenario will be when you become separated form your kayak and cannot reach shore for some reason, such as injury or exhaustion.

Care and Maintenance of Your Gear and Clothing

Surfing can be a destructive environment for gear and clothing. Sand, salt, and sun are powerful aging agents. To maximize the life of garments, rinse them in fresh water to remove sand and salt, and hang them to dry after each use. Store them by hanging them in a cool place indoors, away from direct sunlight. Latex seals on drysuits and drytops can be treated with a specially developed lubricant to keep them supple; otherwise keep them away from heat, and avoid contact with grease.

Check your sprayskirt regularly for signs of tearing, especially where the release tab is connected.

Avoid sitting on your PFD, as doing so will permanently compress the foam buoyancy and reduce the effectiveness and life of the garment.

Oil deposits from beaches can be removed with solvents, but test the effect on a small, inconspicuous area to begin with, in case there is a harmful effect on the fabric or dye.

Rinse kayaks with fresh water, sponge them dry, and store them hanging upside down, under cover if possible, away from sun, damp, and frost. Partly deflate airbags to allow for easy expansion should the temperature rise. Check the security of your footbrace system and end grabs and the condition of your airbags before each use, as these relate to your safety on the water.

Before and after each use, thoroughly check any flares and VHF sets you carry in the surf. Carefully remove end caps from flares and check for moisture. Use a fine smear of silicone grease to help seal end caps. If you are in doubt about the condition of flares or if the expiration date has passed, replace them.

Having the right equipment makes for a great ride.

2 Fitting Out Your Kayak

A poorly fitting kayak can be sloppy to handle and difficult to roll. Making adjustments can mean a properly fitting kayak that is a joy to handle and a breeze to roll. (Refer also to Chapter 6, Essential Kayaker Skills.)

A Basic Fitting

Adjust your footbraces until you can push against them while keeping your knees and thighs gripped against the inside of the deck. Fill the stern with a floatbag or minicell foam so that it cannot swamp, and likewise fill the space between your footbrace and the nose with more flotation. In the event of a swim, this will keep your kayak buoyant and it will be easier to swim it to shore. Full-plate footrests are a better idea than adjustable footpegs. With full-plate footrests your feet cannot slide past, whereas with footpegs a foot can slip off, causing you to lose full control and possibly catch your ankle. If you use footpegs, pack the space beyond with airbag or minicell foam to prevent this.

Glue slabs of minicell foam to the inside of the deck where your knees and thighs make contact. Doing so will add comfort, and the foam can be sanded away with coarse sandpaper to provide a snug fit for your legs. Make sure you can still exit your kayak easily before you next use it on the water.

A Full Fitting

The mass-produced kayak is targeted not at an individual but at paddlers within a range of shapes and sizes, and so tailor-fitting is needed. To "wear" your kayak rather than sit in it can make the difference between fine control with good performance and poor control with unsatisfactory performance: something like the difference between driving a car when the seat is too high, angled too far back, and your feet have to stretch to reach the pedals and driving a car when everything is adjusted correctly. You need a good fit for best control, but your padding can make your kayak more comfortable too.

Following is a range of fitting options. It's not necessary to use all of them; just choose what is useful to you.

Materials Needed

Outfitting Foam

The best and most readily available material is minicell foam. You need foam that is firm when pressed and remains resilient, springing back to its original shape after being pressed. The less dense the foam, the softer and spongier it feels. The greater the density, the firmer and ultimately harder it feels. Less dense, softer foams are more likely to scuff and rip than dense ones, although the resilience is often similar. Foam doesn't come cheap—expect to pay up to $70 for enough foam to completely fit out your kayak. Coarser polyethylene foam (ethafoam) is cheaper and easy to obtain. Although it works quite well, the larger cell size makes cut surfaces more abrasive to the skin and more likely to hold sand, and the foam is less resilient, compressing permanently with use and progressively holding more water. The coarsest grades of foam crush too readily. Ethafoam with a thin skin of minicell foam or neoprene as an outer layer is a cheaper combination with a comfortable finish. Both minicell foam and the cheaper ethafoam can be purchased at kayak and canoe shops and from insulation specialists and packing companies. Some manufacturers offer special custom foam kits for padding out kayaks.

Glue

Minicell polyethylene and ethafoam do not bond easily to the same or other materials. Hence, it's worth spending the necessary time gluing properly so that you do not have to repeat the process too frequently. Use a strong contact adhesive. Seal the surface of the foam where it will be glued by spreading a thin film of glue across the entire area quickly with a broad edge in the manner of spreading butter. Avoid "touching up." Allow the glue to dry completely, then spread a second thin film of glue evenly across both surfaces to be stuck and wait until the glue is just touch-dry before carefully pressing the surfaces together and holding them in position with gentle pressure until the glue has dried completely. Your kayak must be clean and dry for the adhesive to work. It's easy to make a real mess trying to position a piece of foam accurately. Because the slightest touch between the glued surfaces will bond, to help with lining up use a sheet of waxed paper between the touch-dry surfaces. The paper will pull out easily, allowing you to stick the surfaces together gradually and accurately after you have carefully positioned one edge.

Most good contact adhesives take about

THE IMPORTANCE OF FITTING OUT

One rough day in Brighton, one of the kayak club's members, a competent paddler, took out a new club kayak that had been purchased as a shell ready for fitting out. It was just a deck and hull, with the seat fitted and flanges for a footrest. If the club members did the fitting out, the price could be kept down; however, it was a good day, no other kayak was available, and the club member decided to take this particular kayak from the rack.

All went well until on approaching the beach he was caught by a dumper and "beach-looped." As the bow rammed into the beach, he shot down inside the kayak until his feet wedged. Then he was pitch-poled forward. At this point the deck cracked from the pressure, the hull buckled, and the end three feet of the kayak broke away, exposing his feet.

Luckily the adventure ended with no more injury than grazes and a broken kayak. The club member was pulled out of the dumpers and was able to wriggle back out from the kayak.

Waves like these require a properly fitting kayak.

twenty-four hours to cure fully. For best results leave the kayak for the full curing time after gluing, although in an emergency you generally can use a kayak without problems after only a few minutes of drying.

Tools

A band saw will cut clean edges from dense foam as if it were wood, but if you do not have access to a band saw, a handsaw or a stiff-bladed serrated knife, such as a bread knife, will do the job. Use coarse sandpaper, such as 10 or 20 grade, for fast shaping, and use finer paper of 40 or 60 grade for smoothing out the foam. You can sculpt foam quickly using a beltsander, but hand-shaping works too.

Time

I find I need to set aside quite a lot of time for a fitting. Once I have washed and dried the kayak, I expect to fiddle around with the fitting for at least a couple of days to get a truly comfortable fit. Every stage takes time, and tasks such as gluing consume time between coats of glue and cannot all be done at the same time. Choose a period when you will be able to resist the call of the waves for a few days.

Fitting the Foam

1. Begin with a back support, with a rough fitting of the footbrace. Then tailor the side supports for your seat and the knee or thigh bracing. Fine-tuning the position of your footbrace comes last.
2. Now for the footbrace and back support. To handle a kayak well, you should be able to brace with the balls of your feet against the footbraces at the same time as you are clamping firmly with your knees or thighs on the inside of the deck. You should also be able to straighten your legs along the bottom of the kayak comfortably, with your feet upright but without your hamstrings feeling stressed. If you can comfortably alternate between the two positions, the footbraces are well adjusted. If you cannot straighten your legs, the braces need to be moved away from you slightly. If you cannot grip with your knees and/or thighs while bracing with your feet, the braces need to come closer. If you cannot comfortably get into both positions because your knees need to bend too high to reach the deck (this brings the footbraces too close to allow you to straighten your legs), then you need to pad the inside of the deck in the knee and/or thigh area. In this event straighten your legs so that your feet brace firmly but comfortably against the footbrace with your feet upright. Now bend your knees and brace with the balls of your feet. The space between your knees and the deck can now be padded to give you comfortable contact.

3. For surf kayaking a bulkhead footrest is the best option. It is available in the upgraded version of many whitewater and surf kayaks and is well worth the extra expense. Padding a bulkhead footrest will give more cushioning in the event of the nose hitting the bottom during a nosedive in shallow water. An alternative is to fill the whole nose of your kayak with minicell foam to give a solid but cushioned foot support.

4. Even a comfortable seat will seem dreadful if the footbraces are too close, pushing you too far back in the seat. Such an arrangement leads to lower-back pain and leg pain too. A support for your lower back, together with a correctly adjusted footrest, will give you the same seat position every time. A backstrap will give you a firm and comfortable support. Choose one with a broad padded band and with upper attachments to hold it up toward the deck. Think what will happen when you enter the kayak onshore in a hurry. The less the strap can twist out of position, the better, and it should certainly not be able to slip down under your butt if you get shaken around in the surf. Once you have fitted your backstrap, check again that you can comfortably put your legs into the straight and the knee-braced positions. You may find that the back support or the footbraces need fine-tuning to give you better comfort. If the distance from your footbrace to your back support is even a tad too short, the seat will be very uncomfortable or even painful after a short time on the water.

5. Once you have adjusted your footbrace and back support, pad out the inside of your deck

for comfort and better control over your kayak with your legs. You should be able to brace firmly with your knees and/or thighs on the inside of the deck while bracing with the balls of your feet against the footbrace. Generally your padding will be an extension to the thigh bracing already in the kayak. Pad it deeper than you need, then shape away the excess to give the ideal slope, shape, and fit. A small hill of foam between your legs on the front of the seat can also help with your bracing control; however, when you have completed the job, make sure you can slide in and out easily.

6. When I lean my kayak, I slide across the seat until my hip rests against the side of the seat. The less I slide, the better the control I have over my kayak. If my hip supports are too tight, though, my hips will become sore through rubbing when I make the usual twisting actions inside the kayak while paddling. I need a narrow space between hip and side support. The measure is difficult to estimate if you change clothing a lot. A space the thickness of your finger to either side is a reasonable guideline. Fit foam against the side supports of the seat to give you this fit. For best grip shape the foam to overhang your seat somewhat so that it con-

tours your hip. Don't take this to the extreme where it will hamper your getting in and out of your seat or to the point where your hips haul at the overhang when you exit.

7. If you find that your hip rubs excessively when you paddle, use a coarse sandpaper to pare away the foam just in the area of contact. On the market are adjustable hip pads that can be strapped to the side supports of a hung seat; the foam is enclosed in a shaped nylon bag. These can be a good option, especially if several paddlers will use your boat, as thin layers of foam can be removed or added each time for a tailor fit.

Testing and Fine-Tuning

Once you have fully fitted your kayak for comfort and control, make sure you can still exit without difficulty. Paddle it for a while before you make further modifications. Before fine-tuning consider carefully where you need to trim or add padding. For example, what could be corrected by lowering the front of the seat might be better tackled by trimming the thigh brace. Trimming the foot support will have an effect similar to but not the same as trimming the back support.

3 Waves

A "sea"—the spawning ground of swells.

A wave is the neatest package of energy. Light, too, travels in waves. Maybe someday we'll figure out how to surf lightwaves.

How Waves Originate

Without waves there would be no surfing. Where do waves come from? Usually waves are caused by the wind or by a fast current of water. Wind first forms tiny wavelets that travel at the speed of the wind. Known as capillary waves, these create the patterns by which we recognize the approach of a gust of wind across the water. In time, however, a series of larger waves build that travel at a slower speed than the wind producing them. When a wind is blowing, we estimate its speed by how rough it makes the water and by the size and behavior of the waves. This effect on the water is known as a *sea*. A sea is typically chaotic, with waves varying in not only their direction of travel but also their size. The effect is messy and less than ideal for surfing. When a weather system contains strong winds blowing in one area, the waves set in motion will continue to move outward from this center in all directions. As they move through the water, the waves straighten up and become more

Swells.

what provides us with the finest waves to ride is swell arriving on a suitable beach.

Predicting Swell

How do we predict swell? Swell is caused by a weather system elsewhere. The stronger the winds generated by a weather system, the larger the swell will be. Thus the swell produced by a tropical storm over the Atlantic off South Carolina, for example, will be smaller than the swell caused by a hurricane in the same location. Such swell will take several days to reach Connecticut, where there may be no wind at all when it arrives. Exactly how long the swell takes to reach a beach will depend on how far it has to travel and what its speed of travel is. Larger swells travel faster than smaller ones. A swell may travel at 25 miles per hour (600 miles per day), reaching a destination 1,200 miles away in just two days.

A tide race.

uniform, as waves moving in other directions move away. When these more uniform waveforms—termed *swells*—reach shore, they can produce the evenly shaped waves we seek for surfing.

Sometimes we encounter waves created by a current running over an obstacle or through a constriction. Such waves are often chaotic but occasionally form into well-shaped swells. We find such waves on whitewater rivers and also on the sea, where rapids are called *tide races* when the constriction causing them is in the width of a channel and *overfalls* when such constriction is in the depth.

In some locations estuaries funnel a rising tide into an increasingly narrow channel, forcing the mass of water higher. This creates a wave or series of waves behind which the water level is higher than the water level in front. Called *tidal bores*, such phenomena consist of just a few fast-moving waves that move upstream. They will pass only once with each rising tide and only on a few rivers around the world. The tidal bore on the River Severn in the west of England produces a wave up to 6 feet high that runs upriver for some miles.

Although it is possible to ride storm surf, tidal bores, waves in overfalls and tide races, and swell,

Paddling with the stream in a tide race. You surf against the stream.

This time span gives us an easy way to forecast surf, using national weather reports that chart the progress of weather systems large enough to produce swell—although, of course, the direction a beach faces may expose it to or protect it from swell from a given direction.

Look at a national weather chart and locate the positions of areas of low pressure: the *depressions* that spawn waves. Within these areas of low pressure, look for closely packed isobars that indicate a steep pressure gradient and strong winds. Because winds blow counterclockwise around areas of low pressure in the Northern Hemisphere and clockwise in the Southern Hemisphere, almost parallel to the lines of isobars, you can work out whether there is a strong wind blowing in your direction that will send swells toward you. Given that swells will travel in the range of 15 to 25 miles per hour, you can calculate the approximate time of arrival. Surf information lines, however, are often available to provide us with more accurate local data about the conditions in a particular area or on a specific beach. If you need to travel to get to a surf beach, information from on-the-spot reports can save you a wasted journey. Timing can be important. On occasion I, misjudging the timing of the arrival of swell, have journeyed to a beach to discover a calm sea in late evening but excellent surf conditions by the following morning.

Sets

Waves traveling together often catch up or interact with other waves traveling in the same or different directions. Often these waves are from some other weather system or are smaller waves spawned earlier by the same weather system, but they can arrive at your beach at the same time. The bigger the wave, the faster it travels, and so larger swells will catch up with and overtake smaller ones. The distance between crests is related to the speed and height of the wave. Thus if one crest coincides exactly with a smaller one, combining to create an even larger crest, the next big wave will be slightly out of sync with the smaller counterpart, combining with it a little closer to the beach than the previous one—and so on, through a cycle, until you get a series of waves in which the large crests coincide with the troughs of the smaller waves, almost canceling each other out. What you view from the beach is a series of waves, each larger than the last, then fading, wave by wave, to a period in which the waves are much smaller. The large series is known as a *set* whereas the period of smaller waves is known as a *lull*.

Why Waves Break

What makes a wave break? A beach's profile will determine how approaching swells behave. Swells begin to steepen when the water movement within a swell starts to drag against the bottom. This friction slows the base of the wave, while the top continues to move at its normal speed. Ultimately the crest will overbalance and the wave will break.

An even but steep underwater beach gradient with a swell approaching head-on will cause the wave to steepen and break in a short distance. Typically such a combination will produce a hollow wave face, and as the wave breaks, it will pitch out in front of the face, often forming a *tube*—that is, a space between the face of the wave and the falling crest. (If the room inside the tube is sufficient to continue surfing, it is sometimes known as the *green room*.) A ride on such a swell will be fast but short. A shallower gradient with

MORE ABOUT BREAKS

Waves feel bottom when their depth is less than half their length. Once they feel bottom, they slow down, become closer together, and steepen. If a wave's length is 50 or more times greater than its height in deep water, then the wave will also increase in height when it reaches shallower water. The wave will steepen until the water is 1.3 times the height of the wave at that time, when it will break. Onshore winds will cause a wave to break in deeper water, perhaps even in water twice the wave height. With an offshore breeze old swells with a long wavelength can be held up until the water's depth is less than three-quarters of the wave's height.

A tubing wave over a steep beach gradient. The space inside is the "green room."

A gentle break caused by a gently shelving beach.

the same swell will allow the wave to hold up for a longer distance before breaking. Commonly the crest will roll down an easy-angled slope, allowing the surf rider more time to ride the wave over a longer distance.

A swell approaching from an angle to the same beach will break at the end at which it arrives first, breaking across the beach until it reaches the farthest end. This situation is ideal for a surfer: a wave that can be ridden from one end of the beach toward the other while still on an unbroken face.

When a ridge of sand runs out into a bay, the swell will break over the ridge first, again providing a steep spot next to the broken water for the rider to surf, but this time on both sides of the ridge. Because of refraction the wave will curve around toward the ridge from either side, concentrating its energy over that area. The wave will grow larger at that point and break more powerfully there than farther along the beach in either direction. (For more on refraction see page 21.)

Viewing a Beach to Assess Surf Conditions

When you arrive at a surf beach, watch the waves for a time to find out how they are breaking. Watch to see how frequently big sets arrive and how far out from shore they are breaking. Doing so will give you an indication of how much time you'll have to paddle out during a lull, and how far out you will need to paddle to get beyond the break. I have arrived at a beach in a hurry to get on the water and paddled out through the

break to sit offshore to wait for larger waves, only to spot swells much bigger than I had expected breaking well out from where I was waiting. It pays to watch for a while to see how large the waves are in the big sets and in what part of the beach they break first. Then you'll know where to wait to begin the best rides.

Estimating Wave Height

Try to judge how big the waves are. As a surfer, learn to measure wave height as that part of a breaking wave that is surfable. This measure is approximately the top two-thirds of the wave's total height from trough to crest. The slope of the bottom third is so gentle that it cannot be ridden. When you view a wave from the shore, the bottom third also looks steep, because of the foreshortening effect. When you get out there, however, the space between waves is actually made up of this gentle one-third slope. Hence if your wave appears to be 3 feet tall from the beach, the ridable slope is about 2 feet high. Although this may sound small to begin with, if you surf straight down a wave and run ahead of it, or execute a bottom turn in your kayak, a wave 2 feet high will be overhead. (For more on bottom turns see page 72).

Watching for Rips

Rips, sometimes termed *runouts*, are streams of water running out through the surf from the shore. They are caused by the broken water *(soup)* that is carried toward the shore now flowing back out to sea to equalize the level. Rips commonly flow out along the ends of a bay and at intervals along the beach. The heavier the surf, the more

Soup carries water toward the beach.

The water escapes as a rip.

powerful and the more numerous the rips. Watch for a break in the line of swells approaching a beach. Where a rip occurs, the swells will be slowed down and typically will reduce in size, appearing smaller but more chaotic. The rip may measure only 20 yards across but will extend well out past the breakline. Also watch for a stream of water flowing along the shore feeding into a rip that runs out to sea.

Experienced paddlers use rips to help themselves paddle out. The rips provide relatively effortless routes through the surf, with few waves breaking powerfully compared with other locations. But exercise caution, for it's easy to inadvertently get into the zone where the waves are huge and there's no simple way back except by riding them. In big surf rips have been measured at rates up to 20 knots. Swimming and sometimes even paddling against the flow of a rip are ineffective. If you find yourself out of your kayak in a rip, swim across its path and then, when out of its grasp, toward the shore. Avoid rips until you have mastered the wave-riding techniques that will bring you safely back to shore.

The plumes from this "closing out" wave indicate an offshore wind.

Wave Refraction

When waves approach a coastline at an angle, one end of the swell will feel bottom first and slow down, causing the waves to bend round toward the shore, a process known as *refraction.*

Refraction can cause waves to bend 180 degrees around a headland to reach a beach that you might expect to be protected from the swell. Shoals and sandbanks also cause refraction, changing the direction a wave is heading and causing powerful breaks in localized spots.

Imagine a swell approaching straight into a semicircular bay. The length of the swell to begin with will be the diameter of the circle, of which the bay is a half-circle. As the wave refracts to approach the shore, it will diverge until it breaks all the way along the shore. The shore, measuring half the circumference of the circle just mentioned, is longer than the wave was when it entered the bay. As a result of the divergence, the wave diminishes in size as it approaches the beach.

Tip: On really wild days, look for a long narrow bay where divergence will reduce wave size at the beach.

By contrast, picture a wave approaching a shoal. The wave to either side refracts to wrap

A dumping wave on a steep beach.

around the shoal. Inshore of the shoal the swell is no longer straight but horseshoe-shaped, with each side of the horseshoe closing toward the other. This bunching up of the wave at this point will increase its size and may cause it to break here earlier than elsewhere. This phenomenon is called *convergence.*

How Wind Affects Breaks

How do different wind conditions affect a wave's break? With no wind a wave will break when its depth is about 1.3 times its height at that time. An onshore wind will cause the wave to break sooner, sometimes in water of a depth twice that of the wave height. A wave breaking with the wind behind it has less power than the same wave held up by an offshore breeze.

An offshore wind will hold up a wave, making it break later than normal and sometimes holding it up until the wave's depth is less than three-quarters of its height. Thus a 6-foot wave might break into water less than 4½ feet deep; if you perform an ender (tumble end over end in your kayak) here, you will almost certainly hit the bottom. (For more on enders see page 74.)

Finding the Best Surf Waves

Predicting swell is one thing, but finding the best place to surf is quite another. Surf will be biggest on beaches directly facing the oncoming swell; a beach facing southwest will have the biggest waves when the swell is coming from the southwest. If you want bigger waves than these, seek a point where convergence will increase the wave size. If you require smaller swells or a cleaner shape, look for a place where the waves have been refracted around a headland or breakwater to a beach facing a different direction.

An offshore breeze will hold up waves, helping to straighten them into steep walls, whereas an onshore wind will cause the waves to tumble earlier and be less well formed. Choose a beach where the breeze is gently offshore rather than onshore. A likely place to look is a beach behind a headland where waves have refracted around to a beach with an offshore breeze.

Beach profiles will vary with the state of the tide. Get to know your local beaches by studying them at low water, when all the troughs and ridges are visible. Try to surf a beach during the tidal period when you know the profile will give you well-shaped waves and a uniform break. Local knowledge is priceless. A particular beach may experience the best conditions during the middle period of a rising tide and have calmer winds in the early morning, with wind typically increasing as the day progresses. Calm wind conditions will give you smoother wave surfaces to ride, whereas a wind will create a less pleasant chop on the wave surfaces. Ask local kayak surfers about the best places and times, check out local surfing cafes for advice, or team up with other paddlers to investigate the best spots.

4 Beach Safety

Rips, rocks, undertow, dumping waves, tree trunks in the surf zone—all are common hazards. So too are currents, tidal streams running along the coast, cold water, and other people using the water. A surprising number of injuries, mostly minor, befall paddlers. Some paddlers are hit by their own kayak when they are swimming or handling the kayak in shallow water; others underestimate the energy needed to swim to shore through surf.

There is no doubt that surfing can be dangerous. Yet we can safeguard against many of the dangers by being aware of them.

Spikes from dead trees present a hazard on this Florida beach.

Checking Out the Beach

Learn to check the beach for hazards. Inspect it at low tide for rocks, as well as the signs of scouring that can indicate a strong undertow. Often clearly marked at low tide is the position of the rip, showing as valleys or riverbeds running out to sea. A sandbank with a channel running around it to either side will indicate the position of two rips. When the whole bank is covered, the rip will run across the beach inshore of the bank, then more directly out to sea. The direction it takes along the beach will be affected by the direction of the wind (the water will flow stronger with the wind) or of any alongshore tidal stream or current. Rips run stronger throughout the

falling tide and in general are strongest throughout the midtide period of a falling tide.

Look at the beach profile. The slope of the sand in different places can tell you a lot about how waves will break at different levels of tide. A steep incline at any point will be a position over which waves will *dump* (break suddenly and explosively), and a long, gently rising slope will produce a much more even break. Commonly the profile steepens toward the top of a beach, indicating that the waves will dump on the shore around high tide, particularly during spring tides. Spring tides are the larger tides that occur around every full and every new moon throughout the year. The stronger gravitational pull of the moon at these times creates a greater tidal range: The tide rises higher up the beach and falls lower. Neap tides—the smaller tides that occur around the time of a half-moon—produce a slower rise and fall of tide. Surf conditions change less rapidly through the rise and fall of the tide during neaps, and typically the shore break at high tide is gentler than is the case during spring tides.

If the beach contains rocks, note their position relative to shore features that will be visible at high tide, so that you can identify their position when they are submerged. Draw a plan of the beach as you see it, and copy this plan several times for different levels of tide. Note how you expect the waves to break and where the rips are for each stage. As the tide rises, see how accurate your plans and notes are, and analyze any inaccuracies.

Find out the high- and low-tide levels, and check tide times. Local tide tables and a nautical chart for the area will provide you with the information you need. Check for current and tidal-stream information for the coast. Currents and tidal streams will carry you along the coast, especially when you are beyond the break. Because tidal streams can run at several miles per hour, research them first or you may find yourself carried around the next headland. I remember one winter, years ago, surfing a reef break in the south of England and swimming. The tidal stream carried me out around the headland into bigger breakers over rocks. My companion spotted and rescued me, but I was helpless by myself in the current. Had I known better, I would have checked the direction of the tidal stream, figured out which way I would be carried if I got into difficulties, and chosen some other place to play!

When you study the tidal streams, calculate where you would end up as a swimmer and where your kayak might end up if you became separated. Your kayak could get carried ashore by the surf or offshore by an offshore wind, while you were carried along the coast by tidal stream or current. The more aware you are of the overall scene before you head out into the surf, the safer you will be.

When you are out in the surf, use *transit points* to position yourself—that is, line up two objects, such as a beach building and a flagpole, to give yourself a reference line. Every time you realign those objects, you will be on the same line in the surf. Try to identify transit points you can use for the downwind or down-current limit to the area you will surf. Doing so will give you an easy reference to gauge your alongshore drift. It's very easy to become so absorbed in surfing that you watch only the waves and get carried progressively farther and farther along the beach. Be aware!

Dealing with Debris in the Surf Zone

Small debris, such as seaweed, in the surf zone can be irritating: You can roll up draped like Neptune in swathes of kelp fronds. But larger flotsam is more dangerous. In Washington and Oregon in the Pacific Northwest, large logs often float into the surf zone. These logs, weighing many tons, roll in the surf and are as dangerous as rocks. When they reach shore, they are heaped by high tides onto the upper part of the beach, where they present a real hazard only when the tide is high. But every year people are killed by logs moving in the waves at high tide. The water is power-

Logs littering a high-tide line in Washington State.

BEWARE OF JELLYFISH!

Jellyfish are plankton, moving with the currents in the ocean. The ones with tentacles are the ones that usually sting. Offshore winds, which push the surface water from the shore, set up the deeper onshore currents that can carry jellyfish into the surf zone. If you encounter problems with jellyfish, consider moving to a beach that has an onshore breeze.

ful enough to lift and move these massive logs, so keep well away from them, avoiding such beaches when the tide has risen to the point where waves have nearly reached the logs at the top.

Handling a Waterlogged Kayak

When you swim with your kayak, push it along holding one end and keeping seaward of it so that it is not lifted onto you by a wave. In shallow water the soup will carry a kayak sideways with enormous force. Keep your shins out of the way. The backwash will carry your kayak in the opposite direction—that is, out to sea. Again, watch out for your shins. When you have reached shallow water, align your kayak with one end pointing out to sea at right angles to the approaching soup. Stand beside the kayak and roll it onto its side to drain most of the water from the cockpit before you retreat to the beach to complete the draining.

Injuries occur from trying to avoid capsizing in shallow water. Resist the temptation to reach out a hand or paddle to the bottom to try to prevent the capsize; such an action can result in a dislocated shoulder. Instead tuck forward flat against the deck and allow yourself to capsize. Once upside down, you can continue the roll with the flow of water helping you, pushing up against the bottom if necessary.

Locating Help

Although surfing need not be a dangerous sport, accidents do happen, so find out where the nearest help is. Consider how you might summon

emergency services. Find out where the nearest phone is, and identify the location to which you would summon help.

Although comprehensive coverage of first aid is beyond the scope of this book, in many cases even a little knowledge of first aid can make a big difference in the outcome of an accident. You should be aware of the causes, symptoms, and treatment of hypothermia; know what to do with someone who appears to have drowned; understand what best to do or not do with a victim of a dislocated shoulder; and be familiar with first aid for bleeding. Beyond these a course in outdoor first aid is valuable training for anyone venturing into the outdoors, irrespective of the activity. (For further first-aid information see page 29.)

Surfing Buddies

When you begin surfing, you will probably capsize quite a lot. While swimming your kayak to shore is part of the normal learning process, it also helps if somebody is onshore watching out for you and there when you land to reassure you, help you empty out your kayak, and relaunch you. If you paddle as a group, begin with half the group surfing at a time, with each person on the water paired up with a partner on the beach. This *buddy* onshore should specifically observe his or her partner in the surf, watching for a capsize, a swim, or inadvertent straying into a rip or too close to rocks. The buddy should also watch for successful maneuvers. With such a buddy each surfer can receive feedback upon returning to shore, and the partner can learn much by watching from the shore.

Spotters

Besides buddies there should also be at least one *spotter*, a person who keeps an overview of the complete group. By not being so involved watching any single surfer, the spotter can also watch out for weather changes, keep an eye on equipment left on the beach, and be responsible for any group safety equipment. The spotter does not have to be a surfer.

As a spotter looking out to sea, you will experience significant glare from the water in bright weather. Sunglasses, a hat with a brim or visor,

RIPS AND ROCKS

It was a windy day, and the cliffs confining Cable Bay gave just sufficient shelter from the wind to allow the swells to shape up. Outside the bay today the wind whipped the spray from a confused sea. On truly rough days a rip forms in the center of the beach, limiting the surfing potential, but today just the normal rips appeared along the rock to either side. Getting out was easy. The rip on the sheltered side of the bay was like a river, and so with little effort we could get right alongside the biggest breaks, then drift downwind among them to catch a ride back in. (I gain a certain pleasure from working the elements economically.) I surfed till I was spent and headed home.

Later that evening I heard of the misadventure. Some less experienced surfers had used the bay. While they were trying to paddle out from the center of the beach, through the main break, the wind had carried them progressively downwind into the corner of the beach. Two capsized there. The rip on the downwind side of the beach was, if anything, more powerful than the one I had been using, and the pair were quickly carried out to sea despite swimming hard. To add to their problem, the wind kept pushing them toward the rocks at that side of the bay and kept them in the rip.

The surrounding coast is made up of low cliffs, with sharp igneous rock. It was onto these rocks that the pair were finally brought ashore, with the aid of throw lines. Neither the swimmers nor their craft escaped injury.

This type of situation can be caused in a couple of ways, and it presents lessons we can learn:

1. *Before going afloat you should check the position of any rips. You should operate close to the upwind end of the beach, well away from the next rip and well upwind of any rocks, thereby allowing sufficient space for a swim to the beach in the event of a capsize. You need to know about rips.*

2. *These paddlers may have been farther upwind to begin with. Unless you make a strong effort to paddle into the wind, you will always drift downwind while paddling out. Unless you constantly check your position by looking around you at landmarks, you will not know how quickly you are drifting.*

3. *If you get carried into a rip, you need to swim across it to escape. If the rip is against a headland, there is only one way you can swim: away from the rock. Don't put yourself in a situation where a swim away from danger will be against the wind. In this scenario at Cable Bay, the only help that could be given was from the shore, and fortuitously the group was carrying throw lines that could be used from shore to effect a rescue.*

and binoculars may ease your burden. You will also need to dress for the conditions.

If you have no surfing companions, at least take with you someone who can watch from the beach. Should anything happen to you, someone will be there to raise the alarm.

Hand Signals

When you and your companions take turns on the water, you'll need a reliable way of communicating with one another. Work out a system whereby the surfers each check with their buddies at the end of every run, locating them on the beach and giving a thumbs-up sign with an arm held out to one side so that it is visible from shore. Surfers should then wait for a responding signal from their buddies before heading back out into the surf.

As a buddy I like to use a thumbs-up or thumbs-down signal to indicate a good or bad run respectively. I outstretch my arms to the sides and rock my hands to indicate "I've seen better!" I use a single hand held up straight to recall the paddler to the shore and a side-to-side wave to attract attention. I extend a paddle overhead to make these signals more visible if necessary. Sometimes doing so makes it easier for a surfer who may be looking at a beach that is full of people or is backed with logs and branches that make just an arm difficult to distinguish.

As a spotter I use similar signals. To single out a particular paddler, I use a side-to-side wave of an upstretched arm, while pointing my other arm directly at that paddler. I can direct her or him along the beach in a particular direction by indicating the direction with an outstretched arm, or toward a particular spot by direct pointing, or in to the beach by an upstretched arm. You can, of course, add to your repertoire of signals or devise your own system, but all concerned must be attentive and understand and act on the signals when they are given.

Coping with Weather Difficulties

Offshore Winds

An offshore wind will hold up swells longer, thinning the walls until the light shines through with sometimes dazzling clarity. When these waves break, the wind accelerating up the face catches the spray and lifts it like a plume into the air to fall back into the following trough. On sunny days we see rainbows in these plumes.

Bubbly "egg-box" clouds indicate strong winds, sometimes with tornadoes or waterspouts and usually with lightning and rain.

Yet offshore winds can be deceptive. Generally they are stronger farther from shore, and while you wait for a big set, you may be drifting quickly out to sea. Because you will have to push against the wind to regain the shore, try to measure your drift using transit points to the side of the bay, and keep paddling shoreward to maintain your position rather than sitting and drifting. If you capsize and exit from your kayak beyond the break, make sure you retain hold of your kayak or it will soon be blown out to sea with an offshore wind, perhaps faster than you can swim.

Lightning

In many fine surfing areas, thunderstorms can arrive with great speed. Watch out for high towering clouds and dark skies, and take heed when weather reports warn of thunderstorms. A good rule is to leave the water before the strikes of lightning come as close as 5 miles—that is, an interval of twenty-five seconds between flash and crash. Sound travels 1 mile in every five seconds. There is every chance that the electrically active cloud extends closer than the latest strike. If the last strike was just 2 miles away (ten seconds

There is no safe place on the water during a thunderstorm.

between flash and crash), the next strike could be overhead.

An average of 93 deaths and 300 injuries have been reported as a result of lightning strikes every year in the United States, with activity around water accounting for 40 percent of the deaths. More canoeists die of lightning strikes than of any other cause. In one Florida storm alone, the weather department counted 10,000 strikes! Thunderstorms are a real danger. When you see one approach, get off the water fast, before the storm reaches you. Dodging lightning is difficult; it travels at 186,000 miles per second.

If you are caught on the beach in a storm, choose a position part way up a slope, such as dunes behind the beach. Lightning normally joins the cloud with the closest points on land; thus ridges, peaks, and high spots are poor places to be. Electric current follows cracks, gullies, and pools along paths similar to those of flowing water, so avoid such "drainage" paths too. Sit or crouch on some insulating pad, such

as your Personal Flotation Device (PFD). Keep your hands on your lap, your knees up, and your feet tucked close to you. Keep your contact points with the ground close together so that any current passing through the ground will, it is hoped, pass through nonvital parts of the body. You may get uncomfortably wet and cold, but you will reduce the risk of being struck. If you begin to feel a buzzing sensation as a storm approaches, don't just stand around; if you do nothing else, get into your tucked position.

Fog

Though fog is not uncommon in surfing areas, normally the danger of getting lost in fog is lessened, because you can usually find the shore by following the waves. Nonetheless, it is impossible to gauge your drift in fog, and so you might find yourself on another part of the beach when you land. Likewise it is not safe to surf in fog when you cannot see where other people using the water are. If you know there is a chance of fog, carry a fluid-filled compass as a precaution and decide what course you will follow to shore if the fog gets thick. Otherwise keep a watch for the approach of fog if you are in a region where it is common.

Storm Safety

1. Always get a weather forecast. If storms are predicted, be alert for the buildup of thunderheads. Look into the wind for approaching changes.

2. Get off the water quickly and seek shelter in a car or house, or adopt the crouch position.

3. Lightning is instantaneous, but sound travels at only 1 mile in five seconds. Count the seconds and divide by five to discover how far away the latest strike of lightning was. Less than twenty-five seconds and you shouldn't be on the water—the next flash could be much closer.

4. Strikes of lightning often stun rather than kill. Keep up to date with first aid, particularly cardiopulmonary resuscitation (CPR) methods. Your ability will not help you, but it could well save somebody else.

Fog—be careful.

First-Aid Issues

Certain situations call for immediate, enlightened action to be taken. Highlighted here are a few medical conditions and an explanation of the basic principles behind the first aid required. The procedures are not complex. You could save somebody's life if you attend a first-aid course and learn properly what to do. Encourage your paddling companions to do the same—you might value their help one day.

The notes that follow are no substitute for up-to-date medical training, and you are strongly advised to take a basic first-aid course in preparation for using such techniques. You also run risks when applying first aid, both of infection and of possible litigation. Get proper training!

Hypothermia

One sunny day in June I was with a party of kayakers cruising on a river. We reached the sea after lunchtime but I decided to practice rolling before eating. There was a chill wind and after a few rolls my kayak felt as if it was full of water. Yet, when I reached shore to empty it, I found it empty. Puzzled, I tried a few more rolls, but again was struck by the instability of my kayak. I landed and began to search for my shoes on the beach.

Luckily a friend spotted me and, noting my pallor and strange responses, treated me for hypothermia. It took some time before I was really aware of what was going on, and despite the heat of a stove and the car heater, I was still shivering thirty minutes later.

The circumstances leading up to the rolling practice contributed to my condition. I had been late to bed the previous night and only had a couple of hours of sleep. I missed breakfast and paddled lightly clad. Rolling in the cold water in the wind was just the final step.

Hypothermia is a dangerous cooling of the body temperature that if no action is taken will lead to unconsciousness and death. The onset is often insidious. The initial signs of cooling are (1) shivering and (2) pallor of the face and extremities. Shivering is the way the body attempts to gain warmth by muscle activity; pallor too is protective, by reducing the blood supply to the skin where heat is being lost in order to maintain the body-core temperature for as long as possible. Act on these initial signs by heading to shore if you are on the water, going somewhere warm to warm up, putting on additional clothing, drinking warm liquids, and eating. If you see someone else shivering, suggest that he or she do the same.

The next stage in hypothermia is an increasing inability to think and act rationally. The signs vary from person to person and from time to time but typically include irrational activity or responses, slurring of speech, and loss of balance. You might spot a paddler who normally has good balance capsizing repeatedly or staggering on the beach. This is where an attentive "buddy" can save the day by insisting on a warm-up break and getting the potential victim to safety.

As the body temperature drops still farther, essential heat is retained only in the body core, consisting primarily of the mass surrounding the spinal column and brain. As this temperature falls, unconsciousness and death follow.

Prevention

The primary aim is to prevent rather than treat hypothermia, by taking sensible precautions, such as wearing adequate clothing for the conditions, making surf sessions brief in cold weather, watching one another closely, and stopping when shivering begins. Sometimes, however, a swim may be too much.

Treatment

Evacuate rapidly to a place out of the cold, if possible, or create such a place by constructing barriers from the wind. Any activity by the victim will result in energy loss; your aim is to reduce that loss. Quickly replace cold wet clothing with warm dry clothing. Encase the victim in an *exposure bag* (a large windproof bag, usually constructed from heavy-duty polyethylene or waterproof nylon, typically 6 to 8 feet long and 3 to 4 feet wide) to cut heat loss; an extra person in the bag with the victim will rapidly warm up the space. A *group survival tent* (a tent shaped like a squat bottomless cylinder into which a group can huddle, pulling the tent overhead and sitting down to create shelter from the wind; body heat from the huddled party soon warms up the space inside) is an excellent alternative, but most work best with several people inside to create the extra heat. Try to create an environment where the air is warm.

Insulation from the ground is important, and both a warm hat to reduce heat loss from the head and a scarf around the neck will help.

Try to feed the victim warm fluid. (Never administer alcohol, as alcohol dilates blood capillaries in the now cold skin and can fatally cool the blood. For the same reason never rub the skin, as doing so will stimulate blood flow to the skin and could cause death.) When the victim is able to take food, feed him or her. It is important to reassure and talk with the victim, keeping the person awake. If the victim becomes unconscious, lay the person on his or her side in the "recovery position" (see page 31) and check that the person's airway is clear. Monitor breathing and heartbeat, and keep the person insulated from further heat loss.

Typically hypothermia from surfing and other water activities is a result of water cooling, often from rolling or swimming, together with windchill. Though the onset can be rapid, so can apparent recovery, which may appear complete within an hour or less; nonetheless even if the victim insists that he or she is fine, the person should not continue surfing, and a medical check is advised.

In summary, then, follow these steps to treat hypothermia: halt activity, insulate from heat loss, create a warm environment, refuel, reassure, and keep awake.

Drowning

Drowning is caused by a lack of oxygen arriving at the brain, resulting in unconsciousness, brain damage, then death. Drowning occurs when the victim ceases breathing. Depriving the brain of oxygen for more than about three minutes will usually result in some brain damage, and for much more than four minutes is normally fatal; however, in cold water the process can sometimes be drawn out to the extent where people drowning in icy water have been resuscitated with no brain damage after as long as forty-five minutes. So get into action immediately with any victim, and don't give up until a doctor has certified death.

First check whether the victim is breathing. If there is no breathing, next check that the airway is clear: There may be an evident blockage, such as false teeth or the tongue swallowed back. Obviously clear any blockage with the patient on one side, so that any vomit will not block the airway.

Lie the victim on his or her back with the head tilted back to keep the airway open. Pinch the victim's nose, raise his or her chin, and get a good mouth-to-mouth seal to prevent air escaping. Blow steadily. The victim's breast should rise while you blow and should fall by itself when you remove your mouth. If the chest does not fall, check again that the airway is clear of blockage and the head tilted back at the neck.

The victim may not have a pulse. If the heart is not pumping blood from the lungs to the brain, there is no point in putting air into the lungs artificially. Check for a pulse at the artery on the side of the neck. If a pulse exists, continue with your resuscitation, waiting for the breast to fall each time before each breath. The smaller the victim, the shallower and closer together each breath should be. A victim your own size will draw breaths about the same depth as you and at about the same rate.

The same principle should be applied if you are to give *heart massage,* or *cardiac compression*—that is, manual pumping of the heart. By pressing on the heart, you can push blood through the valves, emptying it. Removing the pressure allows the heart to spring back into shape again, drawing in blood once more. But first you need to locate the heart. Trace the curve of the lowest rib until you reach the sternum (breastbone) in the center of the chest. From the base of the sternum, measure up two finger widths, then place the base of your other hand firmly on the sternum above the two fingers. Now place the heel of this hand on top of the first. Crouch beside the patient, straighten your arms, and push down firmly on your hands to depress the sternum 4 to 5 centimeters for an adult (for a child this measure should be less). You need to imitate the rate of a pulse by beating at a rate of about sixty to eighty compressions per minute (faster for a child).

Apply cardiac compression for fifteen beats, then tilt the person's head and lift his or her chin to apply mouth-to-mouth resuscitation for two inflations. Repeat the sequence. Check from time to time whether the victim has resumed breathing and unaided heartbeat, at which point carefully roll him or her into the recovery position outlined below.

The Recovery Position

Lie the victim on his or her side with the down-side arm crooked around to support the

On-the-Beach Emergency Equipment

First-Aid Supplies

Triangular bandage
Gauze bandage
Plaster
Adhesive tape
Scissors
Tweezers
Aspirin or ibuprophen
Eyecup and sterile eyewash
Sutures/sterile strips
Sterile wound dressing
Plastic airway (for use in mouth-to-mouth resuscitation)
Surgical gloves

Emergency Kit

- *Duct tape with scissors for basic repairs*
- *Throw line: This should be at least 50 feet long, with a float at the end, and can be used for assisting a swimmer from the grasp of a shore break, where sometimes the backwash can make landing arduous.*
- *In a cold-water area: Hot drink, exposure bag (a large windproof bag of polyethylene or waterproof nylon) or space blanket, sleeping bag, food*
- *In a warm-water area: Sunscreen, water*

Keep your on-the-beach emergency equipment in a drybag to protect it from sand, rain, and salt water.

head so that the person's mouth is angled down (any vomit would run out from the mouth). The down-side leg should be extended, whereas the upper-side leg should be brought up so that the knee is about level with the hip, to prevent the victim from rolling fully onto his or her face. In this position you should be able to easily monitor pulse and breathing and check for consciousness. Keep the victim warm, and if consciousness returns reassure the person.

General Principles

Attract attention, and commence treatment without delay. Send someone for help, with clear instructions as to where help is needed and what the problem is. Keep calm, and enlist the help of other competent people if you need them, perhaps to check for pulse while you apply mouth-to-mouth resuscitation or to deal with well-meaning spectators. Try to establish a relaxed, comfortable rhythm in what you need to do, so that you will not tire quickly.

Any person treated for drowning must be taken for proper medical care, as complications can ensue.

Dislocation

Shoulders appear to be more susceptible to dislocation in surf, which is why the emphasis is always to keep elbows bent when bracing. Ideally a dislocated joint should be returned to its proper position as soon as possible, to minimize lasting damage. You need to know something about anatomy, however, before you start pulling around on a painful body part. I have never replaced a

dislocated joint, but it has been suggested to me that a gentle, steady pull on the part, away from the dislocated joint, combined with deep breathing by the patient, is a good start. After a while the taut muscles may relax sufficiently for the joint to reseat correctly. If you have not received proper first-aid training in this, it is best to leave the joint as is and get the patient to a medical professional right away. In any case it is important for the person to see a doctor to check that the joint is reseated properly.

Bleeding

First aid for bleeding involves applying direct pressure over the wound to prevent the escape of blood. If necessary, use a pad of some sort to spread the pressure over an area larger than your hand. If possible raise the bleeding part, as blood pumps less strongly uphill. Lay the victim down and reassure him or her while help is being sought.

5 Stretching Exercises

My old car never used to run properly until I had driven for about ten minutes. Then it would begin to perform well. It needed a warm-up. Bodies work a bit like that. Stretching before surfing helps ease us into action. We aren't designed to perform best when "cold."

Stretching before exercise will keep you supple and help prevent muscle injury that can occur when you go straight into any vigorous activity when muscles are "cold." Stretching after exercise is, if anything, even more important, for this is the time when your fatigued muscles can more easily suffer damage. The following series of stretches can be used both before and following a surfing session. They are the stretches that Joey Yeaple uses. As an American Olympic-class kayak slalomist and active recreational paddler, Joey gathered these exercises from other international athletes in her field, and they work well for surf kayaking.

You can start the "on land" stretches as you approach the beach in your car or as soon as you arrive. The "in the kayak" stretches should be done as soon as you sit in your kayak prior to launching. After your surfing session use the land stretches again.

The exact sequence of stretches here is unimportant. Try to string the ones you think will be most useful to you into a sequence that you will easily remember, and try to make the stretching a routine.

All these exercises should be done in a similar way. Breathe out when you stretch, as doing so allows you to extend the muscles more. When you reach the extent of a movement, don't bounce against the limit; just hold the position. For repetition hold each stretch position for twenty seconds. Repeat three times on one side, then three on the other.

Stretches on Land

Shoulders

1. Place your palm on an upright surface, such as a tree, a wall, or a car. Your fingers should be horizontal. Turn away from your hand until it is behind you. Walk forward a little until you feel the stretch from the front of your shoulder to your fingers. Hold the stretch position for twenty seconds, then repeat with the other hand.

Shoulder exercise 1.

2. Stand with feet at shoulder width, back straight. Cup your hands behind you, with fingers interlocked. Keeping your arms straight, lift both arms behind you. When they reach the extent of their range, you will probably feel the tension in the muscles behind your shoulder. Hold for twenty seconds, then relax. Repeat three times.

3. Swing one arm, straight and at shoulder height, across your chest. Use your other hand to hold the upper arm, above the elbow, against your chest. Hold for twenty seconds. Repeat with the other arm.

4. Raise one arm above your head, then bend it at the elbow to reach your hand down behind your head. With your free hand reach across your head and grab your elbow. Pull down for twenty seconds. Repeat with other arm.

5. Keeping your arms straight, swing them in circles from the shoulder ten times in a forward rotation and then ten times backward. Your arms should swing alongside you. Keep the movement relaxed and gentle rather than attempting vigorous windmilling.

6. Shoulder shrugs can be started before you reach the beach; they also help relax your shoulders while you drive. Begin with your shoulders relaxed and down. Pinch them up toward your ears as the first stage in the following movements. Then:

- Roll them forward.
- Roll them backward.
- Bring them straight down.

Repeat the series of movements ten times.

Back

Stand astride with your feet shoulder width apart. Keep your legs straight. Bending forward from the waist, reach one hand down to the opposite foot. Reach across the front of your ankle and grasp the side of your heel, tucking your fingertips underneath. Pull to feel the stretch. Hold for twenty seconds. Do three of these stretches on one side, then switch and repeat on the other side.

Shoulder exercise 2.

Shoulder exercise 4.

Leg and groin exercise 1.

Leg and groin exercise 2.

Back exercise.

Legs and Groin

1. Squat down and stretch one leg straight out to the side as far as is comfortable, resting both hands on the other knee. Press down with your instep against the ground to stretch your groin muscles. Hold for twenty seconds. Switch legs and repeat.
2. Now squat on one leg with the other outstretched in front. Hold for twenty seconds. Switch legs and repeat.
3. Stand on one foot. Reach behind you to grab the other ankle with your opposite hand and pull your foot up behind you to stretch the muscles on the front of your thigh. Stand on the other foot and repeat.

Wrists

Many kayakers complain of wrist problems. These two stretches can help prevent them.

1. Stretch one arm straight out in front of you with your fingers upstretched and palm forward. Place your other hand flat across the top of your palm and fingers and pull back firmly. This stretches your wrist and your fingers.
2. Now drop your hand on your outstretched arm so that your palm is toward you. Pull with your other hand in a way similar to the first sequence.

   Repeat both stretches with the other hand.

Neck

Standing upright, tilt your head slightly to one side. Use the hand on that side to reach across your head to touch your ear with your fingertips. Keeping a steady restraining pressure with your hand, press your head up against your hand. Hold for ten seconds.

Note: It is important to use your hand to restrain your head, not to try to pull it down.

Wrist exercise 1.

Neck exercise.

Stretches in the Kayak

1. Sit in your kayak and reach behind on one side. Rotate your torso until you can grab the opposite gunwale of your kayak with your hand. Pull for twenty seconds.
2. Lean forward with a straight back and try to touch your nose to the foredeck. Hold for twenty seconds.
3. Holding your paddle, reach across the deck to hook your blade against the gunwale on the other side of your kayak in front of you. Pull against the gunwale to create the stretch and hold for twenty seconds.
4. Keeping a straight back, walk your hand back on your back deck with a straight arm until you reach the point at which it begins to hurt a little. This stretches your shoulder and arm. Hold the position for twenty seconds.

You can practice these stretches anytime, not just when you're about to surf or have just come ashore. The more regularly you stretch, the more flexible you will become and the easier many of the kayaking skills will be.

Stretches in kayak (exercise 4).

6 Essential Kayaker Skills

While it's possible to develop some paddling skills by just getting out into the surf and playing, it pays to master techniques that will enable you to progress faster and further. Described here are the most useful skills for kayak surfing. I suggest you work through them on quiet days when the surf doesn't tempt you away. When the waves call, just get out there and play!

Two Key Terms

Two terms used in this manual need explanation:

- *Onside: The side of the kayak on which the paddle is being used.*

- *Offside: The side of the kayak opposite the side on which the paddle is being used.*

Capsize and Wet Exit

A confident capsize and wet exit in which kayak and paddle are retained is an essential safety prerequisite for surf kayaking. First practice the exit procedure while upright on dry land. Sit in your kayak with your sprayskirt fastened and your paddle in hand. Imagine you are upside down.

Hold your breath through this procedure until you surface beside your kayak. Bring your paddle alongside your hull, holding the paddle with both hands. Brace your legs in the kayak to hold yourself in.

Keeping one hand on your paddle, run the fingers of both hands around the cockpit rim from your hips toward the front of your sprayskirt until you locate the release strap. Use the release strap to lift the elastic from beneath the cockpit coaming, and follow the elastic around the cock-

pit with your fingers to release it all the way around. If for some reason you cannot find your release strap (perhaps it was tucked inside the cockpit by mistake or has torn off), grip the sprayskirt fabric beside your hip where the cockpit coaming has little curvature, and release the sprayskirt from there first.

With paddle still in hand, lean forward and put your hands against the deck just behind your hips. Relax your legs and push yourself forward out of the cockpit. The movement is like a forward roll; your legs will follow out easily (if you

To exit upright or upside down, run fingers from hips forward to locate the release strap of the sprayskirt. (If you cannot find it, ease the elastic free from the cockpit by your hip.)

Release the sprayskirt, and with both hands against the deck beside your hips, roll out forward.

lean back, you can scrape your shins on exit). Keep hold of your kayak as you exit so that you surface beside it with a firm grip of both your paddle and kayak. Now quickly transfer your hold to the end grab (handle or strap) at one end of the kayak. In surf this will help you keep your kayak end-on to the waves, offering less resistance and enabling you to maintain control of your kayak as you swim to shore through the soup.

Forward Stroke

A good forward stroke is crucial not only to getting out through the surf but also to catching waves.

The Catch, or Start of Your Forward Stroke

When I began paddling I relied on my arms for forward power. It was several years later when I learned that my torso rotation and my leg muscles could actually offer more than my arms could.

Place your blade close to the side of the kayak, as far forward as you can reach, keeping both arms straight and rotating your torso. Your chest should face diagonally across your kayak toward the off-side. The leg on the placement side should begin bent or relaxed, allowing your hip to fall forward a little, while the offside leg should be straight, or "pressured," pushing your hip back a little.

For the best use of the upper-body rotation through the stroke, your torso should be upright, although we sometimes lean slightly forward when paddling fast in a short kayak to keep the nose from rising so much. Some short hulls designed to plane easily will lift at the bow and you will experience considerable resistance at a relatively low speed. At such times it becomes sensible to compromise your most effective forward stroke with an upright torso in favor of a forward lean to minimize the lift at the bow.

Your blade alignment should provide you with maximum grip in the water when you pull back on the paddle.

The Stroke

Press against the footbrace with your onside foot, straightening your leg and pressing your hip back. Pull the kayak past the blade, using torso rotation through straight arms. Your offside knee should relax and bend, allowing your hip to move forward as your onside hip presses back.

The power phase of your stroke should conclude when your blade ceases to be at a good angle to grip the water—that is, when it reaches the region of your cockpit. If your shaft angle falls to forty-five degrees from the water, much of your energy will be expended lifting water instead of powering you forward. Rather than wasting energy in this way, slice the blade edge-first from the water.

The power phase of the stroke is short, and the blade should exit swiftly, ready for the stroke on the opposite side to ensue, unless you need to follow the power phase with a steering or corrective action at the stern.

Course Correction

Course correction is achieved either (1) following a forward stroke, before lifting the blade from the water, or (2) at the bow, before the start of a forward stroke.

The forward stroke: the catch, the end of the power phase, and the exit from the water.

The forward sweep.

At the Stern

Your normal forward stroke should finish by your hip. Keeping your elbow by your hip, slice the blade edge-first from the hip diagonally back until the blade is aligned with the power face toward your stern. Your blade should now be at least 1 foot out from the side of your kayak. Holding the position with your lower hand, push across your kayak with your top hand to lever the blade closer to the stern. This pulls the stern toward the blade and points your bow away from the correction. You make the correction on the right to point your kayak farther to the left.

At the Bow

Place your blade slightly out from the bow at the *catch,* and with the power face angled toward your bow. Pull the blade toward your bow with your bottom hand while pushing across your kayak with your top hand. This pulls your bow sideways, pointing you in a new direction. As your blade nears your bow, curve it around into a normal forward stroke, keeping the power on the blade all the way around. This correction is described as a *bow draw leading into a forward stroke.* It changes your direction toward your power stroke, whereas the correction at your stern adjusts away from the power stroke.

RESISTANCE TRAINING

Your forward stroke should be fluent and powerful. Smooth out any jerky movements until one stroke follows the next in a graceful cycle. Practice on flat water. If you find it difficult to maintain a powerful straight-armed stroke on flat water with no great resistance to push against, try paddling against a resistance—for example, someone holding your stern with his or her kayak dragging behind you at right angles. Such resistance training can more accurately simulate the resistance you might experience paddling against the wind or through the soup.

The Sweep Stroke

The Forward Sweep

The farther from the side of your kayak that you sweep your paddle, the more your kayak will turn. Begin the sweep stroke close to the bow. The first part of the sweep moves the bow away from the blade. The blade must be aligned so that the power face is directed from the side of the bow. Through the midpart of the sweep, extend your reach to bring the blade in a wide arc with the blade as far out as possible, close to the surface. As you finish the semicircle with the blade, angle the power face slightly down toward the water, raising your off-hand. Push your off-hand across your kayak to complete the sweep stroke. At the end of the stroke, both hands will be on the same side of the kayak. During this last part of the sweep, you are pulling the stern toward the blade.

Keep your kayak upright throughout this sweep. Straighten your onside leg and press against the footbrace to power the kayak into the turn.

The Reverse Sweep

For the reverse sweep use the back of the blade. Reach behind you to place the blade close beside your stern, with the back of the blade angled slightly down against the water. Push the blade out from the stern in a wide semicircle to finish close to the bow. Use torso rotation to power the stroke, driving the turn by pushing

The reverse sweep.

against the footbrace on your offside and relaxing your onside leg.

Alternate between a forward sweep on one side and a reverse sweep on the other in order to spin your kayak on the spot.

Edging

Edging is tilting your kayak sideways while keeping your body in balance. Edging is an essential technique to give directional and turning control when surfing.

Lift one cheek of your butt and push all your weight onto the other. Keep balance by arching your body sideways. You will be able to edge far-

Edging. Keep your body weight over your kayak.

ther if you rest your head on your shoulder on the side of the kayak you are raising. Straighten the leg on the side you are weighing down, and lift the knee of the side you are raising.

Braces

You brace when you use your paddle to maintain your balance. Bracing can be precautionary, like holding a handrail when climbing steps, or it can be used as a recovery to bring yourself back into balance, like grabbing the handrail to prevent a near fall.

The Low Brace

The low brace is a good technique to prevent yourself from losing balance when you practice edging. It is also the way to stabilize yourself when you feel unsteady.

THE HIGH BRACE VS. THE LOW BRACE

U*se the high brace to recover your balance when you lose it, and use the low brace to stabilize when you think you might lose your balance. The low brace, using a pushing-down action, will work only when your elbow is above the paddle and the back of the blade is on the water.*

Place the back of the blade flat on the water beside you. Bend your arm at the elbow above the shaft so that you can push powerfully down against the water with the blade. Be careful not to overextend your arm: You risk damaging your shoulder if your elbow is straight when you brace.

Now hold the blade just above the surface and edge your kayak toward the paddle. At the point of balance, press down on the blade and simultaneously lift the knee of your straight leg and drop your head toward your knee as it rises. This jackknife effect will right the kayak abruptly and leave you in a stable position, with a low center of gravity. This abrupt movement, often called a *hip flick,* is essential also to both the high brace and the high-brace roll.

Position your blade level with the cockpit for maximum leverage. The farther aft you place the blade, the closer to the center line of the kayak it will become and the less leverage you will have.

The High Brace

If you lose your balance, you may drop below the limit of effectiveness of a low brace. The high brace, with its pulling-down action, will work even if you turn completely upside down but is awkward to use when your kayak is still just in balance. You need some commitment if you are to practice this technique.

Use the power face of the blade. Keep your elbow immediately beneath the paddle. Lift your onside blade high, but keep your offside hand close to or touching the offside of your kayak. Edge until you lose your balance. When your blade hits the water, pull down on it and "hip-flick" to right your kayak.

You can practice the hip flick by holding the bow of another kayak. Lie in the water with your head on the surface and your kayak inverted. Pull down on the bow of your assistant's kayak. Keep your head on the surface while you jackknife your body to bring your kayak upright and your hip to your head. Finally, keeping your head low, bring your body upright.

Turning on the Move and Steering

Depicted here are two ways to turn on the move.

The low-brace recovery.

To fine-tune this turn, use only a short initiation stroke from the bow so that crossing the paddle over to brace on the opposite side is straightforward. If you carry your sweep too far back, the crossover will become awkward.

The Bow Rudder

The bow rudder is a useful stroke for controlling your direction when paddling out through waves and is a quick way to turn to catch a wave while maintaining forward speed.

The high-brace recovery.

The Low-Brace Turn

Paddle forward in a straight line. Initiate the turn by performing a short forward sweep on the outside of the desired turn (on the left side if you want to turn right). Brace on your paddle on the inside of the turn. Place your blade either (1) level with your cockpit for maximum leverage and security or (2) farther aft if you wish to incorporate something of a reverse sweep at the same time. Either way your blade should be almost flat on the water, with the leading edge raised slightly so that the blade planes across the surface in the manner of a skimmed stone. Your kayak will pivot around your paddle.

Edging will make your kayak turn quicker and aid your stability. Edge into your turn—that is, lean your kayak into the turn as on a bicycle.

The low-brace turn.

The bow–rudder turn.

As with the low-brace turn, you will need forward speed. Initiate the turn with a short forward sweep on the outside of the turn. Now place the paddle alongside your cockpit just ahead of your torso, on the inside of the turn, with the blade's power face toward your kayak. If you are moving forward, no resistance to either side of the blade should occur in this position. Adjust the pitch by rotating the blade to bring the leading edge farther from the kayak than the trailing edge. This brings water pressure against the power face, drawing the blade out from the side of the kayak. Resist this pull to make the bow turn.

Getting the blade into position can be awkward. Begin as with a forward power stroke but without the power, so that the kayak glides past the blade. When the blade reaches your hip, rotate the paddle into the neutral position, where no pressure exists on either side of the blade. Now increase the pitch until the power face is catching the flow. Alternatively drop the blade into the

water in an arc beside you. Begin with the power face toward the stern and quickly slice the blade past the position when the face is toward the side of your kayak into the bow-rudder position.

A bow rudder is used for turning out to sea.

Bow-Rudder Tips

The more upright you can get your paddle, the more effective the bow rudder. If the shaft is angled across your kayak, the blade will lift in the water, losing its hold on the water. Position your top hand directly above your bottom hand by rotating your torso (straightening your leg on the inside of the turn and relaxing your other leg) and pushing your top hand across your kayak at shoulder height for maximum reach. Your bottom hand will be close to if not touching the water. As you turn toward the paddle, increase the pitch of the blade to maintain its grip on the water and pull the blade toward the bow. Keep a hold on the water by pulling the blade around in an arc, pushing out from the kayak with your top hand, until the blade is in the starting, or catch, position for a forward stroke. When you now complete the forward stroke, it will stop the turn and power you forward. In this way you exit your turn with control and speed.

The bow rudder is a perfect way to pull off a wave at the end of a ride.

Steering

Steering a straight course can require effort to prevent turning. You can steer only when you are moving, so practice on the move.

The Stern Rudder

Align your paddle to one side and parallel to your kayak. The blade should be about 1 foot from the side of your kayak. Rest the back of the trailing blade on the water and raise the outer edge higher than the edge closest to the kayak. In this position your kayak will turn toward the paddle. Now raise your front hand and drop the elbow of your trailing hand toward your hip so that your trailing hand is higher than the elbow. The power face of the

There are three positions for the stern rudder. Use the first one to track straight. To turn toward the offside, angle the power face of the blade against the water. To turn toward the onside, angle the back of the blade toward the water.

blade should now be catching water. Maintain pressure on the blade by pulling down with the trailing hand and pushing out from the side of the kayak with your top hand. Your bow should now turn away from the paddle.

If you place the blade behind you in a neutral position where the water is catching neither side of the blade, holding the shaft alongside the hull, then the kayak will track straight.

Practice these skills on flat water until you master the subtlety of each, becoming adept at steering your kayak a few degrees to one side and then back again until you run out of speed. The stern rudder is the most frequently used method of steering on the wave, although in positioning and blade presentation it is most often a cross between a low brace and a stern rudder.

Rolling

Rolling is easiest learned on flat water, preferably in a swimming pool, but rehearsing the movements on dry land may cut down on the time you need to spend in the water before you are successful.

Body Movement/Hip-Flick Exercises on Dry Land

First make sure your kayak is adjusted well to fit your legs and feet. When you sit in the kayak, your feet should brace firmly against the footbraces, while your knees should brace upward and outward against the inside of the deck. Too loose a fit will result in not enough control, whereas too tight a fit will cause your legs to go to sleep and could be painful to both your legs and your lower back. Rolling will press your knees against the inside of the deck quite hard, so glue in foam padding if necessary (see Chapter 2, Fitting Out Your Kayak).

Find a soft area of ground. Lie out to the side of the kayak with your shoulder on the ground and your paddle blade on the ground in the high-brace position. Invert your kayak so that your body is bent sideways. This is the position you should adopt in the water at the start of a high-brace roll. (For more on high-brace rolls, see page 52.) To roll up, pull down on the paddle and perform your hip flick, as described under "Braces" earlier in this chapter.

The set-up for a roll: Paddle alongside the kayak.

Bring the paddle out at right angles to the kayak and raise it to the surface. Lean toward the paddle.

Keep your head down while you flick the kayak upright.

Bring your body and head out of the water last.

When you capsize in the surf, you should tuck your paddle close alongside your gunwale to prevent its being taken from your grip by the force of water. Practice this now, on dry land. Invert your kayak as before, tucking your paddle alongside the gunwale while holding it in your normal handgrip. Now lift the rear blade across your inverted hull to position the front blade out to the side as before, ready for a high brace. This is the movement you need to make underwater to get into position for a high-brace roll.

Eskimo Rescue

For an Eskimo Rescue you will need to work with a kayaking partner. Here you will pull up on your partner's kayak instead of using your paddle. The exercise is a good way to practice the hip flick from underwater and helps you get used to holding your breath and waiting in an inverted position. In surf you frequently need to wait for the kayak to stop bouncing around in the turbulence of a wave before you roll up.

The capsized paddler:
1. Grips into the kayak with thighs, knees, and feet.
2. Leans forward until forehead almost touches the deck and extends one hand to each side of the hull into the air to bang on the hull to attract attention.
3. Moves hands slowly backward and forward beside the kayak, approximately 1 foot from each side.

The rescuer:
4. Approaches at speed, turning and slowing to present the bow to the waiting hand.

The capsized paddler:
5. Grabs the bow and lifts head to the surface to breathe, pausing a moment to concentrate on correct body movement, then flicks upright.

Note: The capsized paddler should keep the paddle alongside throughout, pinned between arm and body.

Body Movements for the Roll

Two alternative body movements can be used with a roll, as can a few in-between ones; described here are the "C to C" and lie-back styles. Which style you use will probably be determined by the kayak you surf and by your bodybuild. A surf kayak with a low-volume stern, for example, will stand on end if you roll it with a lie-back, but some paddlers find the lie-back the easier body movement to master; hence I describe both styles below.

The "C to C"

This movement is sometimes described as a hip flick. Start with your body arched sideways. When you are underwater, this position will bring your body close to the surface; this is the first "C" curve, to one side. Now bring your head forward and toward your knee on the opposite side. Simultaneously pull your knee up against the deck toward your head. (Alternatively bring your head sideways toward your hip, finishing with your nose close to your armpit.) This movement rights your kayak and brings your body into the second "C" curve.

Practice this movement sitting on the ground. Sit upright on the floor with your legs in front of you as if you were sitting in a kayak. Now lean over to one side and put your elbow on the floor, about the length of your forearm from your hip. Roll your legs with your knees together until the side of one knee touches the floor. This is the simulated "capsized" position.

Now jerk your butt into the sitting position, keeping your elbow on the floor and dropping your head until your cheek rests close to your shoulder. This is the hip flick that rights your kayak. It now remains for you to bring your body upright, sliding your forehead as close to the ground as possible until it is over the kayak.

In water lean to one side as far as you can to position your head close to the surface, allowing your Personal Flotation Device (PFD) to float you up toward the surface.

The Lie-Back

Practice this movement on dry land first. To begin, get into the simulated "capsized" position as described above. Now rotate your torso to lie with your back flat on the ground, and arch your back, lifting your hips. This movement is used to right the kayak. Keep the back of your head as close to the ground as possible as you swing your body around until it lies arched back across the rear deck of your kayak.

Paddle Movements for the Roll

Get used to tucking your paddle alongside your kayak when you realize you are on the way into the water. It is easiest to control your paddle here so that it does not get wrenched by the water. Tuck the paddle to the side on which you enter the water—for example, tuck toward the left if you are capsizing toward the left. Whatever force makes you capsize will almost certainly help you if you roll completely rather than surfacing on the side you fell in. Keep your normal grip on the paddle. This is the *set up*, or starting position for the paddle after capsize.

The High-Brace Roll

Variously called the *put-across* or the *"C to C,"* this technique is most easily understood as a high brace started underwater.

From your setup position lean well over toward the surface and toward your paddle and lift your whole paddle out of the water horizontally. Swing the rear blade beneath your seat until your paddle lies out at a right angle from your hull. Push the outermost blade (the one that was the front blade) toward the surface until it breaks the surface; the power face should be flat against the water. Now, to right your kayak, pull vigorously down on the blade and perform either the "C to C" or the lie-back body movement.

The Sculling Roll

This technique is variously called the *screw*, the *reverse screw*, or, with an extended paddle, the *Pawlata* or the *Styr*, depending on whether the scull begins as a forward scull or a reverse scull. But because I advocate continuing to scull until you are upright, *sculling roll* seems a simpler and more descriptive name.

From the setup position upside down in your kayak, angle the blade to skim across the surface by rolling the palm of your front hand forward toward your wrist, so that the blade sets at a similar angle to the deck on that side of the kayak. Lift the rear blade out of the water and tuck it beneath the hull behind you. You need to do this to ensure that the back blade clears the hull when you roll.

Now sweep the front blade out in an arc toward the stern of your kayak. When the paddle reaches an angle of about forty-five degrees from

the stern of your kayak, reverse the scull to skim across the surface toward the bow. Again change direction to a forward scull as soon as you reach an angle of about forty-five degrees from the kayak. (The closer your blade is to your kayak, the less support you will get from it, so keep the blade away from the gunwale.) Your elbow should be bent and hanging below your paddle shaft. The leading edge of the blade should be raised slightly to provide lift as it skims the surface. Make use of this lift to flick your kayak upright with either the "C to C" or the lie-back body movement.

IMPROVING YOUR ROLL

1. *Tuck your paddle alongside your hull on the side you will enter the water as you capsize.*

2. *Always, before you begin your roll, lean your body toward the surface on the side you hold your paddle. Doing so saves you the effort of dragging your body through the water into that same position using paddle power during the roll itself.*

3. *If your roll is unsuccessful initially, try to retrieve the situation using a sculling stroke.*

4. *When you are practicing, if your rolling starts to get worse instead of better, take a break, then go back to rehearsing your body movement without your paddle. Then ask someone to support your kayak so that you can concentrate on perfecting your paddle technique.*

A Deepwater Rescue

A deepwater rescue is a good alternative to swimming in to shore if you are beyond the breakline, but it can occasionally be used during a lull inside the normal breakline if you are well rehearsed, quick, and prepared to immediately abandon the rescue if a breaker approaches.

In this maneuver the rescuer approaches the swimmer, who is holding the bow of the kayak, together with the paddle. The rescuer takes hold of the bow of the swimmer's craft and directs the swimmer to hold onto the bow of the rescue kayak. The swimmer retains his or her own paddle, while the rescuer takes care of his or her own paddle by placing it across the sprayskirt, under the PFD. It is essential that each person keep watch of his or her own paddle throughout.

The rescuer:

1. Lifts the bow of the upturned kayak, breaking the seal of the cockpit against the water, and holds the bow up while the water drains out.
2. Hauls the kayak upside down across the rescue kayak's deck until the balance point is passed and the bow of the draining kayak drops, to allow water to drain from the stern.
3. Flips the kayak upright and draws the two

kayaks tightly alongside each other, facing opposite directions.

4. Holds the cockpit of the now empty kayak, firmly and with both hands.
5. Takes both paddles and pins them across the two kayaks.

Now the rescuer directs the swimmer to:

6. Grip the back of the swimmer's cockpit with one hand and the foredeck of the rescuer's kayak with the other.
7. Lie back into the water, so the swimmer floats on his or her back.

Following a capsize, hold the end grab of the kayak and your paddle.

The rescuer takes the capsized kayak, while the swimmer holds onto the rescue kayak.

The rescuer seesaws the upturned kayak across his deck to drain the water, then flips the kayak upright.

The rescuer slips the kayak into the water so that it is facing in the opposite direction of his own kayak. The swimmer passes his paddle to the rescuer.

The swimmer pulls the kayaks together as he arches up into his cockpit.

The rescuer stabilizes the kayak while the spraydeck is sealed.

8. Lift his or her feet into the cockpit.
9. Squeeze the two kayaks together behind the swimmer as the swimmer lifts him- or herself from the water onto the back deck and straight into his or her seat.

The rescuer must now:

10. Maintain a good hold of the rescued craft until the sprayskirt is properly on and the rescued swimmer is ready to paddle away.

The whole rescue needs to be performed swiftly in surf. Thus when you practice, use a stopwatch and strive to increase your speed and efficiency.

(For rolling under a wave as a way to get out through surf, see Chapter 7; for rolling with the soup, see Chapter 8.)

7 Getting Out There

Arriving at the parking lot overlooking the beach, we used to sit for anywhere up to an hour watching the waves, wondering whether they were big enough to warrant getting cold for. Then we'd get out of the car in a rush, unload the kayaks, change, and carry our craft down the beach. At the water's edge the waves always appeared much larger than they did from the top of the beach. My stomach would drop a little as I launched. Reading the wave patterns to get an easy route out was a mind game in which fear played its part: I really wanted to avoid being annihilated by a big breaker! Even when I had made it out as far as the clean green swells, my anxiety inevitably lingered until I took off on my first ride of the day. Then my grin would widen and my movements would relax. I would come to life again.

A similar apprehension is experienced by many surfers, often caused by the threat of capsize or doubts about swimming in surf. Sometimes it's best to begin by getting wet, deliberately capsizing, and then swimming to overcome that initial doubt before heading out farther.

Trying a Capsize and Wet Exit in Surf

Once you're familiar with the wet-exit procedure as described in Chapter 6 and have practiced it on flat water to the point where you can do it without anxiety, try a capsize and wet exit in the soup. Remember to keep hold of your kayak and paddle throughout the procedure. Swim your kayak to shore.

While holding a kayak in surf can be difficult, a runaway kayak poses a serious danger to swimmers and other surfers. For safety keep hold of it. It will help carry you to shore and will also make you more visible from shore to anyone watching out for you.

Swimming in Surf

Most likely you will swim from time to time until you perfect your roll in surf, and even then you may have occasion to swim now and then. It's a good idea to practice swimming in surf to gain confidence and know what kinds of forces are involved when you swim in breaking waves. Wear your normal kayaking clothing, including a PFD and a helmet. Choose a place where no rip occurs, and first make your way out into the surf, then turn around and swim back.

After a wet exit maintain your hold of both kayak and paddle and move quickly to the seaward side of your kayak to avoid the danger of its being thrown onto you. Minimize the grip of the waves on the kayak by turning it end-on, and push it to shore, keeping to the seaward end. If you do get separated from your kayak, swim as fast as you can to reach it.

Occasionally you will need to get away from your kayak. If you find yourself in tubing waves, or shore dumpers, and a real danger exists of being hit by your own craft, get away from it and retrieve it afterward.

Although deepwater rescues are not often practical within the surf zone, occasionally time allows for a quick rescue in a lull beyond the break, before the next set arrives. In this event be prepared for the rescuer to abandon you at a moment's notice if a breaker approaches.

Launching

Watch the waves for a while before getting into your kayak. Ideally you should time your launch to coincide with the start of a lull. In other words watch while the larger waves of a set break, then prepare to launch when the waves become

Launching, using hand and paddle.

progressively smaller. Because smaller waves will not reach so far up the beach, walk down with your kayak to within a few feet of where the backwash is reaching, quickly slide into your kayak, and fasten the sprayskirt. Now use your hands to push against the beach to slide the kayak into the water. As soon as you float, paddle hard out to sea.

Watch the pattern of waves. If you see an opportunity to paddle straight out through the waves to a point beyond the break, paddle hard to get there. Otherwise wait where the soup is not too powerful until you see an opportunity to sprint out. The best time is usually immediately following a set.

Deciding How Far Out to Go

Ideally you will paddle out beyond the breakline and wait there to select a wave to ride. Your ability to do this, however, depends on the size of the surf and your skill and confidence. What you are seeking are clean green waves rather than soup to ride. Sometimes when the surf is heavy, the waves re-form closer to shore and you can get good rides on the second breakline. Still, nothing beats waiting on the ocean for a big set on a day when you're comfortable riding the biggest waves that are coming along. Most likely you will not perform at your optimum if you are intimidated.

Tackling the Soup When Paddling Out

Paddling through the soup can be hard work. As a beginner you'll spend more time in the soup than a skilled surfer will, but your stamina will increase as a result.

Meet each pillow of water head-on. If you lean back momentarily as the wave reaches your bow, your kayak will rise over the soup more lightly than if you keep your weight forward, and less water will hit you in the chest. But this should be a quick movement—lean forward again and dig in with your paddle as soon as you feel the nose of your kayak rise.

Keep your paddle in a vertical position beside your kayak's bow to get maximum hold and haul yourself through. Unless you tackle it aggressive-

Be aggressive paddling out.

ly, the soup will carry you back to shore. A power stroke close beside the kayak will keep you straighter than one farther out from the side. You need to maintain your direction.

Handling Waves That Seem Ready to Collapse

Inevitably you will from time to time meet waves that will dump on top of you. Try to anticipate where an approaching wave will crest first, and aim for a part that will hold up longer. Ideally you want to get over the wave where it is still unbroken, for the part that has just collapsed will be powerful soup.

Choosing a route out through the surf so that you do not work harder than you need to is a skill you will acquire with practice. Good timing is an acquired skill too. If the wave does begin to collapse as you reach it, tuck your weight forward and roll upside down. A steep wave will often pass clean overhead, leaving you to roll upright again immediately, beyond the wave. A less clean break, where the full power of the soup is already thundering down toward you,

Don't be deterred by breakers. Aim for the unbroken section and paddle hard!

is likely to carry you shoreward upside down for a little way before releasing you. Be prepared to hold your breath, and be patient. Most times you will still have an easier time upside down than upright, and will be carried for a shorter distance. In other words if you really want to get out through a heavy break, rolling under is usually your easiest option.

Using a Rip

Rips will speed you out through the break but will also carry you out if you are in difficulty. Use rips with caution. Check which direction they will carry you by watching the patterns on the water (see Chapter 3), and make certain they will take you where you want to go. Remember, the bigger the waves, the more powerful the rips, so if the surf is huge and you want to go out just a little way, the rip might not be the best way to get there. I have seen surfers make use of a rip and then find themselves intimidated by the size of the waves they are carried to, whereas had they paddled out without the aid of the rip they would have stopped long before they had gotten so far from shore. If used sensibly rips do, however, pro-

vide a good way out through surf. When you are beyond the break, paddle along the beach to find a place to surf in, for the waves in a rip are generally of poor quality.

Board surfers using a rip.

A Strategy for Tackling Steep Unbroken Waves

Head up the wave at an angle and ease over the top gently. If you paddle straight up at speed, you will probably become fully or partly airborne and land with a jarring crash in the following trough.

8 Learning in the Soup

In my early surfing days, I would play endlessly in the soup, never getting out beyond the break. This was my learning ground, and I believe now that this initiation was responsible for my level of kayak control today.

Bracing on the Wave

Surfing sideways by bracing on the soup is a fun and exhilarating way to ride a broken wave—and a good way to gain confidence.

Sit broadside to the soup. As the soup approaches, prepare to brace onto the oncoming wave with a low brace. Keep your paddle shaft as horizontal as possible so that the blade remains flat on the water. When the wave hits, raise the shoreward rail, preventing it from catching in the water as your hull slides sideways with the soup. Keep your elbow bent and raised above your paddle so that you can push down to maintain balance. Keep your blade just ahead of your hip. You will be carried sideways in the soup until it loses power.

Different kayaks will perform differently in this braced position, depending on the relative buoyancy fore and aft. If your kayak turns to surf forward, move your brace farther forward until you are carried directly sideways. Likewise if your kayak turns to surf backward, move your brace to a point closer to the stern. Once you have found the balance position, try a few more waves until you're confident you can always brace in the right place for side-surfing.

Now try the high brace. Again keep your paddle shaft as horizontal as possible. Too steep a shaft angle will cause the blade to grip the water, pulling your arms straight and putting you at risk of a shoulder injury. Keep the blade in a flat position so that it will slide on the water, giving support as you slide sideways. Keep your elbows bent.

When you are confident in both low- and high-brace positions, try switching from high to low and back to high while being carried sideways by the wave. This will develop your sense of balance to a point where you can side-surf with minimum weight on your paddle, or even control the edging on stable soup without using your paddle.

A Learning/Teaching Aid

Work in a pair, your partner standing in waist-deep water where soup is rolling in. Have your partner hold the bow of your kayak until a suitably powerful wave approaches, then spin you broadside. Position your blade ready for a brace (high or low) and let your partner support the blade while you edge lightly. When the soup hits, your partner should let go of the blade, allowing you to slide away. To avoid injury from any sharp edges on the blade when you move away, your partner should sink his or her hands to release the blade.

Structure your session so that you practice both the high brace and the low brace, both to the left and to the right. Working in waist-deep water gives you a clearly defined working area where wave size is limited and any accidental capsize will not result in a long swim. Count your runs and then switch with your partner. Taking turns will give you both the opportunity to watch, which will help you to learn.

When you are both confident with your side-surfing, progress to the next step: steering while side-surfing.

Surfing sideways. As the wave approaches, wait parallel to the wave.

Get ready for a high brace when the wave hits.

A crucial safety point: Keep your paddle nearly horizontal or sloping up into the wave.

Steering While Side-Surfing

You can make your kayak move forward along the soup by moving a high brace toward the stern and leaning back. This weights the stern and unweights the bow, freeing the bow to turn downwave. You can encourage the turn by raising your offside hand slightly so that the blade grips the water a little more, creating drag at the stern. But keep your hands below shoulder level, to safeguard your shoulder.

You can make your kayak surf backward and along the wave by bracing toward the bow in a similar manner and leaning your weight forward. Be particularly watchful over your shoulder when you do this, because while you are concentrating on your paddle position you can move quite fast toward others who are using the water.

Edging is the key!

Switching Sides

You can switch sides during a side-surf by first freeing the bow so that you slide forward along the wave, in a high-brace position as before. Now raise your offside hand to shoulder height and bring the blade into a stern-draw position. Draw the stern gently until you are surfing directly downwave, bringing your weight above the kayak's centerline. Keeping your weight aft to maintain a buoyant bow for turning, transfer to a low brace on the other side, trailing the blade behind you. Edge toward this new side to encourage the turn and bring your blade forward to the side-surf balance point once again.

To complete a 360-degree spin in the soup, follow these steps:

1. Switch sides as above.
2. Bringing your brace forward, lean forward to weigh down the bow and lighten the stern.
3. Bring your paddle slowly into a more upright position and use a bow draw to straighten your kayak for reverse surfing. Keep your weight forward and watch where you are going.
4. Now switch to a brace on the other side, edge toward this new side, and move your brace to the side-surfing position as the kayak turns to complete your 360 spin.

Running Ahead of Soup Straight for the Beach

Wait with your kayak pointed directly toward the beach. As the wave (soup) lifts your stern, lean forward and paddle to accelerate. As soon as your kayak surges forward, stop paddling, lean back, and steer, using a low brace or stern rudder, alternating sides to keep your bow pointing toward the beach. The trick is to use only sufficient energy to catch the wave, then to let the wave carry you. If you paddle too fast for too long, you may outrun the soup and end up paddling to the shore ahead of the wave. Once you have caught the wave, remember to lean back or your kayak will almost certainly *broach* (turn sideways to the wave) or *pearl* (bury its nose).

Turning from a Side-Surf to a Forward Run

The technique you use for the 360 spin in the soup can also be used to regain a forward surfing position from a side-surfing one. Move your brace from the balance point toward the stern and lean back. As the bow begins to drop and you start to slide forward along the wave, raise your offside

PRACTICE RIDES

*B*egin in shallow water (waist-deep), with your partner holding your stern. In this way you can easily maintain your position facing the shore until you are ready and have chosen a suitable wave. As the wave (soup) lifts your stern, lean forward and paddle to accelerate. Your partner can assist you in getting your first rides by pushing your kayak forward as the stern lifts. Working this way with a partner ensures that you begin your practice in waves of a suitable size.

hand to shoulder level and draw the stern sideways, centering your weight over the stern as you continue to turn downwave. Now switch from using the power face to using the back of the blade, switching sides as necessary to steer your kayak toward shore. Trim by leaning forward or backward for optimum handling.

Alternatively, once the "bounce" has gone from a broken wave, balance your kayak without using your paddle, then slip the blade in at the stern on the downwave side. Now lean back and across your kayak, edging it toward the downwave side. As you turn downwave, neutralize your edging and steer with a brace or rudder on whichever side is appropriate.

Rolling with the Soup

Wait broadside to the soup in waist-deep water, over a gently shelving beach. Avoid rocky areas. Capsize away from the approaching soup and set your paddle in position for a high-brace roll with your blade raised from the water. Begin your roll when you feel the wave hit you. The wave will help roll your kayak upright, so brace gently.

Next take a side-surf and deliberately capsize toward the beach. Make the paddle transfer from a brace into the wave to a tucked-in, wind-up position as rapidly as possible so that the blade is positioned before you hit the water; otherwise the turbulence in the wave will make it harder for you to position your blade. Begin a slow roll the moment you hit the water. The wave will do most of the work to bring you upright. Practicing in the soup is a good way to get used to rolling in turbulent water.

Towing a Swimmer

Towing a swimmer to shore is a basic surf rescue technique. Here the swimmer holds your kayak by the stern's end grab, kicking his or her legs to assist while you paddle strongly for shore. The swimmer acts as a drogue, holding you stern-on to the approaching waves. Lean back to keep your bow light when waves hit. If the swimmer loses his or her grip, return to the person as quickly as possible.

PRACTICE ROLLS

*H*ave your partner hold your kayak end-on to the soup in waist- to chest-high water until you are ready to begin. Set up your paddle ready to start your roll, alongside your kayak. Have your partner spin your kayak broadside between the waves, leaving you to capsize away from the approaching soup, toward your paddle. Working with your partner in this way will ensure that you have sufficient depth of water yet are not beginning in waves that are too powerful.

When the "bounce" has gone from the soup, slip your blade in at the stern on the down-wave side, which will steer you along the wave.

Lean back and across your kayak, edging it toward the down-wave side.

As you turn, neutralize your edging and steer with a brace.

9 Riding the Wave

The *wave,* or *green wave* as it is sometimes called, is the swell that is steep enough to ride, before it has broken. It may be breaking alongside you, but while you are on the unbroken section you are "riding the green wave." This is a very different experience from riding the soup.

Selecting Your Wave

Wait for the right wave: Selecting a good one will give you the best opportunity to practice maneuvers. Look for a peak on an unbroken wave, indicating where it will break first. You need to be positioned close to that peak or, if the wave has already started to break, next to the shoulder. If you are not close, wait for another wave. If the waves are always peaking in the same spot, move close to that point.

Select a wave that looks as though it will break progressively, rather than one that looks so regular it will probably collapse over its whole length at once (a phenomenon called *closing out*).

Take Off!

The steep wall of water seemed to grow even taller as it approached. The offshore breeze accelerated up the rippled face with a rushing sound and whipped a fine spray from the crest. It was this wind that made it difficult to catch the waves today. I paddled hard, yet was carried to the very top of the wave.

Suddenly I could feel the hull begin to slide on its own, as the crest began to curl and break. I was almost free-falling. The wind resistance was no longer sufficient to stall me. With my eyes full of flying spray, I was away!

Position yourself close to where the wave will break first.

If the waves are arriving in clearly defined sets, remember that the first wave in the set will probably decline, whereas the third and fourth waves will probably build. Let the first couple of waves pass.

The Takeoff

Taking off in a kayak is a bit like bump-starting a car. First you put a lot of energy into pushing the car to get it moving fast enough, but when the engine fires you can relax and let the car cruise along under its own power.

Although there are several approaches to takeoff according to your position on the wave, take time to perfect this basic takeoff.

Angled Takeoff

If you are close to the break, the wave may be sufficiently steep to take off diagonally, making it easier to escape from the break along the shoulder. The steeper the wave, the easier it becomes to takeoff directly into a diagonal run.

Basic take-off: Select your wave, then paddle powerfully straight downwave until you feel the kayak slide downhill on its own.

Now steer.

Basic Takeoff

Align your kayak at right angles away from the approaching wave, ideally just to one side of the break. Wait until the wave is almost on you before you begin to accelerate. You can reach maximum speed in a few strokes. When your tail begins to lift, accelerate and throw your weight forward. Keep paddling until you feel the wave carry the kayak forward, then trim your weight as necessary and steer away from the break.

An angled take-off: Accelerate away from the break, edge into the wave, and bring your paddle to the downwave side to steer.

Late Takeoff and Bottom Turn

Take off on a wave that is going critical (about to break). You will drop almost vertically, picking up enough speed to carry you straight onto flatter water ahead of the collapsing wave. Edge and perform a carved bottom turn (see page 74) to carry you out onto the face beyond the broken section of the wave.

Faded Takeoff

If you are too far from the break on takeoff, angle your craft toward the peak during your acceleration and initial takeoff, so that you begin in a diagonal run toward the break, turning when you have positioned yourself better. The object of a faded takeoff is to gain a good position on the shoulder as soon as possible.

Paddle-Out Takeoff

Sometimes when you are paddling out, you will see a wave you would like to ride that has already started breaking. Paddle out diagonally toward the break and turn abruptly downwave at the moment you hit the soup. Begin your run falling with the soup, then steer out onto the face.

Control on the Wave

To surf, you need to have control of your kayak, and you need to be able to read the wave and anticipate what will happen next. You also need to love the movements you make. But complete control? No. In the end it's the lack of complete control that offers you excitement and entices you for another ride . . . and another . . . and yet another.

A faded takeoff: Catch the wave diagonally toward the break, then edge downwave and begin your turn.

Now ride the shoulder.

Using a stern rudder to steer a straight course.

Steering a Straight Course Toward the Beach

Once you have caught a wave, the easiest ride is straight toward the beach. Use a stern rudder or low brace on alternate sides to maintain your course. Keep your weight back for easy steering.

Zigzag

Steer straight for the beach, at a right angle to the line of the wave. Now edge toward a low-brace rudder until the kayak turns. Next brace on the other side, and edge toward the paddle once more.

Keep the kayak tracking within about thirty degrees to either side of a straight course toward the beach. Concentrate on making the transition from one turn to the next smooth and fluent.

Steering a Diagonal Run

When you surf diagonally across a wave, your speed far exceeds the speed of the wave! The ability to control a diagonal run represents a breakthrough in your learning progression. It is the means by which you can move along the wave to keep ahead of the break, allowing you the time and space to string together a sequence of maneuvers.

Begin with a straight run toward the beach. Your speed will be the same as the wave's. Now

Steering a diagonal. Practice on both sides. Turn from one diagonal to another.

A MEMORABLE DAY

The storm pounded the swell onto the shore. Most of the Cornish beaches were closed, but although this narrow twisting bay was closed to swimmers, the lifeguard said we could surf our kayaks. The swell in the inner arm was clean. Beautiful swells were peeling left across the bay. Although the shape was regular and the break was consistently right to left, the waves were not very big. We paddled around the corner to see if we could find something bigger.

Outside the bay, the swell was huge. It pounded the headland to either side with a thunderous ferocity, sending spume pluming into the sky. Close to the side of the entrance to the bay, the waves were big and steep, breaking rapidly away from the rock. We scoped it out, then went for it. I was in my surf kayak. It was a little short for the size of wave, for I couldn't catch anything until it was breaking. As the crest dropped behind me, in that moment of quiet before water crashed onto water, my hull skipped and scooted away downhill, thudding across a washboard surface of ripples like a rock across corrugated steel.

Timing was critical. I had to turn diagonally left immediately or the break would envelop me. But the instant I touched the tip of my blade in the water, the kayak skidded round and I was sliding backward. The break immediately enveloped me and cartwheeled me end over end, side over side, in a frenzy. I clung to my paddle, feeling my hair being hauled through the holes in my helmet and the water sucking my sprayskirt against my thighs. When I finally rolled up, I felt weak. But I was challenged—this was not going to be an easy break to master.

I paddled out and had another try. Once again at the falling speed of takeoff, the sensitivity of the planing hull had me spinning the moment I touched the water with my blade. Once again I was trashed.

For a third time I dropped down that wall of water. The hull vibrated across the ripples, and I could feel the forces gather around me. I touched the water with my paddle edge as if stroking it with a feather. I had it! The steering was so sensitive! Moments later I was edging fiercely and carving across the face with the crest thundering down toward me, but I was in the right position. I was able to keep just ahead of the break as it collapsed until I reached the deeper water in the middle of the bay, where I could cut back and work the break.

So now that I had worked out the technique, could I surf more successfully? Apparently not. My success rate that day on that break must have numbered at best one in five. Yet the exhilaration was enormous. When I landed that day, I discovered that the pounding of the hull across the wavelets swarming across the face of that break had cracked my hull from side to side beneath my seat. Even so, the repair work was a small price to pay for such a memorable day.

---

edge and brace to one side to initiate a turn. As with the zigzag, you should now transfer your brace to the downwave side, but don't change your edging. Edge toward the wave but brace on the downwave side. Use your brace to prevent the kayak from broaching, and tuck your weight forward. The closer to a straight run to the beach you steer your course, the easier it becomes to hold a diagonal run, but you'll achieve the fastest speeds when your track is about forty-five degrees to the wave.

To trim your course, adjust your edging and the pressure on your braced blade.

Cutback

The *cutback* is a double turn that enables you to reposition your kayak on the steepest part of a wave.

When you surf a wave diagonally along the shoulder away from the break, you will sometimes outrun the steepest part of the wave and find yourself on a gentler slope. You will slow down. To regain the *pocket* (the steep face right beside the break), turn downwave by pushing your braced blade out from the side of your kayak while transferring to a downwave edged position.

This sequence shows the first turn of a cutback. Rotate your torso to face into your turn.

Flatten your blade and edge into your turn.

Push your blade forward and bring your hips in line with your torso.

Stern rudder on the opposite side and edge into the wave to control your new direction.

A full turn from diagonal to diagonal. This shows the second turn in a cutback.

Pivot around your blade until you have changed direction and are once more edged into the wave. Switch your brace to the downwave side and control your diagonal run toward the break. When you regain the steep part of the wave, make your second turn before you reach the break, edging downwave once more onto a braced reverse sweep and pivoting around the blade. As soon as you have completed this turn, trim your kayak on its original diagonal course away from the break. This double turn is the cutback; use it repeatedly to maintain your position on the steepest and fastest part of a wave.

There are several ways to perform a cutback, adding variety and style to your run, but master this basic one first.

Roller Coaster

The basis of a roller coaster is a diagonal run along a wave. But instead of keeping a straight diagonal course, make use of the wave height and make your kayak rise and fall as you go.

As a basic technique, increase the push against the downwave paddle brace and release the upwave edge to make your kayak drop down the wave, then steer back onto your original course, edging into the wave and ruddering or bracing on the downwave side. For a more flamboyant roller-coaster ride, steer upwave using an upwave brace for a moment, leaning back. As you reach the crest, lean downwave for a moment onto a reverse sweep or brace to turn downwave, applying an edge on the upwave side and ruddering on the downwave side as a diagonal run as soon as you've picked up the necessary speed.

The object is to track along the wave in a series of upwave and downwave turns, making full use of the wave height. The steeper the wave face, the closer to the crest you will be able to steer, to the point where during your turn at the crest your paddle will pull you around while your kayak is airborne for a moment. This is called an *aerial*.

Bouncer

Surf toward the break and make a sharp turn against the soup, leaning downwave onto a brace while you turn. The bottom of your hull should hit the soup. The effect is an extremely quick rebound onto the shoulder, with the hull "bounc-

Climb and drop—the basis of the "roller coaster."

ing" off the soup. The downwave acceleration you can get if you choose to turn and drop straight down the wave can be considerable, because this is the steepest part of the wave. Use this technique to enhance the effect of a cutback.

Floater

Surf toward the break, steering high up the wall so that your speed carries you from the green wave onto the top of the soup. Turn toward the beach and "float" down the falling soup onto the slope below it. Steer diagonally back onto the face, edging into the soup and ruddering on the downwave side.

You can use this technique to cross a collapsed section of wave to gain the shoulder beyond. It provides an alternative to steering across the base of the soup.

A floater has a different feel from that of most other surfing maneuvers. The kayak seems suspended, motionless, a somehow quiet contrast for a moment: a feather falling. When you reach the base of the wave, the sense of speed returns as your hull once more skims across a water surface that feels almost solid.

Bottom Turn

Drop straight down from the lip of a steep wall until you reach the flatter water ahead of the wave, then edge into a turn to take you across and up onto the face once more. To make the bottom turn truly effective, steer your kayak right beside the collapsing soup, then out onto the flat water in front of the soup before turning back onto the face. Try to achieve this without the soup catching up with you at any point.

360s

The 360 spin is a sliding flat spin—imagine sitting spinning on flat snow. You need a steep wave and an actively planing hull. To start, accelerate down the wave from the top. The steeper the wave, the easier it will be to achieve a good spin. Keep your weight centered over your seat, and do not hold an edge. Make a powerful reverse sweep on one side and follow through right away with a forward sweep on the other. Your kayak will skid around. Stop the spin with a stern rud-

A 360-degree flat spin (captured in mid-spin), used here to stall and let the break catch up.

der. You will gain height on the wave during the spin, and so it can be used as a stalling maneuver to bring you back up to the top of a wave. You need a steep wave with some height because a 360 stalls your kayak; otherwise the wave will leave you behind.

The flatter your planing hull, the more easily you will achieve a spin; if, however, your kayak is fitted with fins, you may be unable to perform this maneuver.

Reversing

Surf directly toward shore. Reverse sweep on a trailing blade to spin your kayak into reverse. Lean forward to keep your stern buoyant, and check over your shoulder to watch where you are going. To surf diagonally in reverse, edge into the wave and apply a rudder at the bow, with the power face of your blade angled down on the downwave side.

Finishing Your Run

You can finish your run in several ways, depending on the wave. Typically you will try to ride the wave for as long as possible without being caught by the break. But when you have ridden the shoulder to the point where it no longer has sufficient power to permit an imaginative continuation of your run, edge hard into the wave, bracing upwave, then apply a bow rudder to turn the kayak up the face and over the lip for a crisp exit.

The easiest way to finish a run is to aim for the beach, lean back, and wait for the soup to carry you shoreward. Then, ride the soup.

Pulling off a wave at the last moment. Edge hard onto a high brace and as your bow turns to face uphill, bring the paddle forward into a bow rudder. Keep your blade in the water to follow your bow rudder with a forward power stroke to pull you through the crest.

With a wave about to close out, turn upwave, using the same bow rudder or bow draw and keeping your weight forward as you make the transition from a bow draw to a forward power stroke. This is a deliberate and precise turn off the wave. Timing is crucial; leave it till the last minute but not a moment longer or you'll be caught by the break. Practice this finish as your standard exit from a wave.

Alternatively perform a bouncer against the soup ahead of you, and as you pull out of the turn climb immediately, using a bow rudder, edging hard into the wave, and holding your weight well forward.

Another exhilarating option is to climb the face as if to exit but then turn sharply downwave when you reach the crest. Your aim is to drop from the lip as the last section of wave collapses. Lean well back; the power of the soup in this collapsing section will thrust you forward at high speed. Your positioning and timing are what will make this maneuver special. Make the turn too soon and you'll have reached the bottom of the wave before the crest topples. Make it too late and you'll be enveloped in the break before you have a chance to turn downwave.

Riding the Soup

Many maneuvers can be performed in the soup in the same way as on an unbroken face. You can use these to extend your run toward the beach, or use the soup for practicing particular maneuvers and general kayak control in turbulence. (Refer to Chapter 8 for information on basic in-the-soup control.)

A Diagonal Run in the Soup

Use the wave as if the soup weren't there. Because the soup is likely to make your kayak leap and buck, edge hard while keeping your blade braced on the downwave side so that you have a firm supporting grip on the water for balance.

Turn from a diagonal run to the opposite diagonal by pushing harder on the brace as a sweep and releasing the edge to allow the hull to spin freely.

If you incorporate a downwave lean, you can engage your downwave edge as the kayak turns. The result? A tightly carved turn in place of a hull-spinning turn.

360s in the Soup

The 360 in the soup is a good way to practice hull-spinning turns. Begin on a diagonal run, with your paddle braced downwave and holding your upwave edge. Release your edge at the same time as you push sharply against your brace. This will cause your hull to spin. As soon as you have completed your reverse sweep, begin a forward sweep on the opposite side, to keep the kayak spinning. Your forward sweep will end with the blade near the stern on the upwave side as you

complete your 360. Angle the blade into a high brace if necessary to stabilize yourself. Now edge into the wave and redeploy your downwave stern rudder or brace.

Reversing in the Soup

Surf directly toward shore. Reverse sweep on a trailing blade to spin your kayak into reverse. Lean forward to keep your stern buoyant, and check over your shoulder to watch where you are going. To reverse diagonally, edge into the wave and apply a high brace into the soup on the uphill side of your bow.

Tailspin in the Soup

During a reverse diagonal run, throw your weight back and simultaneously pull your blade in a forward sweep from its position at the bow into a high brace. This movement is designed to bury your stern and stand your kayak on its tail. Lean your weight toward the braced blade and continue your forward sweep on the brace to twist your kayak through 180 degrees while it is on end. Finish in a forward surfing position, regaining your diagonal run as smoothly as possible by edging into the wave and applying a downwave stern rudder or brace. Although a turn can be made in a flat spin, planing throughout, this more difficult move combines a reverse ender with a 180-degree paddle-controlled spin.

Acrobatics

Ender

An *ender* is a maneuver in which you turn your kayak end over end. Although it's difficult to regain a wave following an ender, you can use an ender to exit a run. It is also fun to practice in isolation on days when the quality of wave will not permit satisfying rides.

To perform an ender, you use the fact that a wave moves through the water, whereas the water remains where it is. You ride a wave by sliding down the slope, but if your nose buries, the water in which it buries is not moving. If the angle at which you bury your nose is sufficient for the water pressure to hold it, and the wave is power-

The author in the early 1970s performing a forward ender.

A reverse ender in the soup. Begin with your weight back

ful enough to carry you forward regardless, then your kayak will be thrown on end.

To bury your nose, you will need (1) a steep angle of fall, (2) speed, and (3) your weight held forward.

First you need to travel fast on a steep wave. An ideal situation is to perform the first turn of a cutback and steer diagonally toward the break. When you reach the steepest part of the wave, make your second turn, but at the moment you face directly downwave, throw your weight forward to encourage the nose to bury. When the nose buries, remain folded forward and the wave will carry your stern into the air and over your bow. You will end up upside down, facing out to sea; thus prepare to roll when the turbulence ceases.

Popout

Begin your ender at speed from a steep wave to get maximum penetration. Keep your weight well forward, but as the kayak approaches verti-cal, lean back so that you stand on your foot-

Here the power of a small breaking wave is used to lift the kayak on end.

A forward ender. Lean forward to begin, then backward, to hold the kayak on end.

brace and delay the kayak in the upright position. Now the water pressure on the bow will squirt the kayak upward. If you had sufficiently powerful penetration, the kayak will be squeezed completely out of the water on end. This is a *popout*. With a good popout the kayak can leave the water by several feet. As the kayak falls forward, tuck your body forward once more, ready for landing, so that you do not injure your back on impact. Hold your paddle firmly alongside your gunwale so that it is out of the way when you land and is in position for starting a roll.

Pirouette

Begin as for a popout, but as your nose buries, set your paddle alongside your kayak as if for a roll (see page 50). When the kayak begins to rise

The Early Days of "Beach Looping"

I began surfing in the southeast of England, where steep shingle beaches, made up of rounded flint pebbles, cause dumpers at high tide. When I joined the Brighton kayak club, the better paddlers used slalom kayaks with built-up balls of fiberglass at the bow. These kayaks were scarred from bow to cockpit, with cracks from side to side across the deck caused by "beach looping"—their term for standing their kayaks on end on the shingle beach. The method was to sit just beyond the break, where the dumpers gathered their strength. The backwash from a wave would suck back with a roar of rolling flints to expose the beach right at the base of the building wave. A couple of paddle strokes at the right moment and a lean forward would set the kayak's bow onto the shingle, when the wave would burst apart and push the kayak upright.

It was a nice concept, but I found the flaws one by one. When I got the angle slightly wrong, I would be pitched sideways onto the pebbles at the base of the wave and the wave would dump with all its power right down on top of me. Usually a successful beach loop would result in a lingering period

with the kayak balanced on end. The maneuver would conclude in a face-first fall toward the beach. By this time the pebbles would be covered with the swash from the broken wave. By tucking forward against the deck, I would be washed up the beach into water shallow enough for me to flick myself upright. At that stage I had not yet learned to roll.

On one occasion in quite small dumpers, I paddled to the beach to greet a friend who was standing at the water's edge on top of the steep pebble bank. Eager to impress, I timed my arrival perfectly to coincide with a small dumping wave and promptly stood my kayak on end. Then I realized that the swash would not reach more than a couple of feet up the steep bank. I flattened myself against the back deck and stared with wide-eyed horror into the face of my friend only a few feet in front of me. Any moment now and I could topple forward to land on my face on the beach. Luckily I eventually fell backward instead, leaving my friend with a long-lasting tale to tell of the terror in my face as seen from a distance of a couple of feet.

on end, use the blade in the same way as you would with a roll, to twist the kayak. The result will be a spin like a top. How far you manage to spin around will probably depend on your skill on the trampoline. A spin of 180 degrees is fine, for this enables you to land upright facing out to sea, but I once saw a paddler achieve 540 degrees several times in a row. He used a vigorous body twist, throwing hands and paddle around toward his rear deck as he rose.

Acrobatics in Reverse

Surfing in reverse can be fun and stimulating; it can add interest and challenge to your surfing day. But be aware that you cannot see where you are going as well in reverse as forward. Be careful for the safety of others. Reverse enders carry the risk of jarring your back against the cockpit coaming and can be particularly dangerous in water shallow enough for the stern to touch bottom. A good back support in your kayak will help, but your back will not survive impact as well as your legs will.

Putting it All Together

Once you have mastered a number of moves, you are then in a position to link them together to make a run. In competition you will be judged on the variety and number of maneuvers you can string together on a single wave, as well as your artistry in making the performance flow smoothly with style. If you are surfing for your own pleasure and not in competition, trying to make the same full use of every wave you catch can be very satisfying.

When you practice stringing together moves, it helps if you can repeat certain sequences until they are seamless, then add moves before or after your sequence until you include a good variety in each ride. The following sequences can be used in that way.

Try these:

1. Choose a steep shoulder on an unbroken wave. As soon as you have caught the wave, ride toward the point you believe will break first.

2. When the wave breaks, position yourself as close as possible to the soup, then turn away into a diagonal run.

3. Hold your diagonal course until you have outstripped the break, then turn back toward the break and make the second turn of the cutback as close to the soup as possible.

4. Now run away from the break in a roller coaster, rising and falling on the wall.

Try this more difficult version of a cutback:

1. From a diagonal run away from the break, turn and run diagonally toward the break.

2. At the last moment before reaching the soup, climb to the lip, then turn sharply downwave, leaning and edging onto a low brace so that your hull hits the soup (this is a bouncer). At this point you will be edging on the downwave side through the turn.

3. As soon as your nose is pointing toward the beach, remove the edge on your kayak and continue to push your blade toward the bow to maintain your turn, setting your kayak into a flat spin.

4. Continue through 360 degrees. Exit the 360 (actually more like 450 degrees in total) crisply into a diagonal run across the shoulder away from the break.

As an alternative to the second turn of a cutback, run diagonally toward the base of the wave beneath the break. Turn upwave at the last moment to run uphill into the soup. Edge into the wave. Stall by bracing against the soup, then reverse onto the face, controlling with a bow rudder into a reverse diagonal away from the break. Turn (still in reverse) to reverse diagonally toward the break. This time when you hit the soup, brace until you have control, then rudder at your stern on the downwave side, edge into the wave, and run diagonally forward onto the face again.

Faded takeoff.

Diagonal toward the break.   *Sharp turn from the break.*

Steering on upwave side in order to turn and climb.

Diagonal away from the break.

Cut back to keep close to the break.

From a diagonal, turn downwave to drop.

*Edge into the wave on an upwave brace
to climb again.*

Trimming for maximum speed.

Edging hard into the wave to maintain a diagonal track with the intention of regaining the face.

10 Miscellaneous

Wave Etiquette

Several "rules of the road" have been established for surfing with other paddlers and board surfers. These serve to maintain a level of safety in the break zone and also avoid confrontation by establishing certain rights-of-way on the wave. Some of the unwritten rules are common sense; others require an understanding of wave riding before they make sense. If you follow the guidelines, you should be able to surf responsibly without upsetting others.

A quality surf spot is rare and so attracts the most surfers. If waves are peaking at a particular spot time after time, this is where the surfers will

Understand Your Fellow Surfers

Surfing recently at Westport in Washington State, I rode the rip out beyond the break, only to receive a stream of shouts from local surfers on boards. One came over and began telling me I was a liability and should get myself well down the beach, out of the way of the boards. To my mind this was a reasonable request, because for me to use the rip to get out and then to paddle along to the next excellent break was easier with paddles than it would be for a "boardie"—and besides, I'd have a clean break with no competition, while the competition for the break nearest the rip was fierce with a lot of boards. Still, I wondered at the attitude of the surfer. He explained that he had been going out when a kayaker came riding in "out of control" and ran into him. When he complained, the kayaker had arrogantly shouted, "Well, you should have gotten out of the way then!"

On a crowded wave, who has the right of way? What strategy should a kayaker adopt?

wait. It will be a busy place when the swell is good, and competition for a ride on a good wave will be keen. To make poor use of a wave and deprive competent surfers of the chance to ride good waves would be discourteous, so don't use busy quality spots to learn boat control; use them only when you're good. Surfers of all kinds generally respect good surfing but can be abusive or aggressive toward riders who spoil the rides of others, especially if a rider does so through lack of control, ignorance, or selfishness. *Dropping in*—that is, catching a wave that someone else is already riding—is bad, it spoils properly set-up rides.

Here, two surfers catch the same wave. Who has the right of way?

Answer: Both. Each surfs away from opposite ends of the break.

As someone in a paddle-powered craft, you'll be able to catch waves earlier and more easily than board surfers, who have to be in precisely the right position at the right time before they can catch a wave. Be courteous and don't hog the waves.

Rules of the Wave

1. When you are paddling out, keep out of the way of surfers riding waves; take evasive action. When there is a rip or established route out, and a "best" section for riding in, use the established route and don't paddle out in the area where surfers are riding in.

2. In general the first rider to catch the wave has the right-of-way.

3. If two or more riders catch the same wave simultaneously, the one closest to the break, on the steepest part of the wave, has the right-of-way. Other surfers should keep out of the way or pull off to give the rider with the right-of-way enough space to maneuver.

4. Once a surfer is riding the wave, others should not try to take off closer to the break. The wave is taken!

5. A surfer has caught a wave when he or she has ceased paddling and the kayak is planing on its own.

6. If a rider takes off on a completely broken section, that rider has no right-of-way.
7. A rider gains the right-of-way if he or she surfs from the broken water onto an unoccupied face, but not if it is occupied.
8. A rider must avoid all swimmers, stationary surfers, and people paddling out. As a rider you must pull off, capsize, or take evasive action to avoid others in the water.

In essence if you are surfing "in the pocket" close to the break, you have the right-of-way over all the surfers on the same wave that are surfing farther from the break and over surfers who have not yet caught the wave. If someone is riding the wave closer to the break than you, you should pull off to leave the wave to that person.

Surf Competition

What's it all about?

Surf competition is the kayaker's equivalent to freestyle dancing competition, or gymnastics. There is no easy way of measuring the winner of a competition; it is more the subjective decision of a panel of judges. Usually about four paddlers are in each heat, with the highest-placed going on to the next level until the final is reached.

The judges will be looking for the following:
1. *Wave choice.* How good is your wave selection?
2. *Wave reading.* How good is your positioning on the wave? Are you staying close to the shoulder? Can you anticipate how the wave will develop?
3. *Length of run.* How long is your run on the unbroken wave?
4. *The maneuvers themselves.* How many were executed? Did they demonstrate range and variety? How well were they linked?
5. *Personal flair and style.* What is the overall polish and individualization of the performance?

Strive for a flowing performance that combines a variety of maneuvers on the fastest part of the wave. The better your positioning in the pocket, the better you string maneuvers together, the more competently you perform moves, and the more inspired your performance, the higher the judges will mark you.

You will have only limited time to show what you can do. Start by getting out through the break. Only rarely will you collect marks without starting beyond the break.

Next choose your wave. You will have time for just a few choice rides and will be scored on your best five. If you catch fewer than five, you are unlikely to be in the running, but a poor wave will give you a bad start. Wait for a good one so that you can achieve a good takeoff. Inasmuch as others will be competing at the same time, make sure you wait in the best position to have the right-of-way on the wave. Now perform as many different moves as you can, keeping as close to the break as possible. Finish your run cleanly and deliberately—you don't want to get taken sideways to the shore. You need to make best use of your limited time by paddling straight out again and choosing your next wave.

You will score higher for a perfectly executed maneuver than a poorly executed one. You will score higher for a maneuver performed in a good place on the wave; for example, a 360 spin executed just 5 feet from the break will get a better score than the same spin executed 30 feet from the break.

At the end of your twenty-minute heat, your score will be calculated by adding the total marks from your five highest-scoring runs. This figure is then compared with the other competitors' marks, and the surfer with the highest marks wins the competition.

Throughout the competition safety is of utmost consideration. Go to the aid of a surfer in trouble rather than completing your ride.

Whether or not you decide to compete, surf competitions are good places to get inspiration for trying new maneuvers and identifying different surfing styles. If you are there to watch, take binoculars and clothing suitable for standing around on the beach.

The Psychology of Surfing

I didn't feel so good that day. There was nothing I could blame for it, nothing I could pin it down to, but I felt uneasy and I think I should have listened to my intuition earlier.

My friend Ray and I launched at Soldier's Point on the north end of Holy Island and paddled our whitewater kayaks around the coast toward the cliffs of North Stack. Here the tidal stream rushes around the headland and over shallows, causing overfalls that can be spectacular. Today the waves were chunky and breaking heavily—we could see that from a distance. It was the conditions we had been hoping for. As we drew closer, the pull of the tide made our work easier; the tide here runs in excess of 6 knots.

We ran into the tidal rapid with whoops of excitement, bouncing through the exploding "haystacks" and colliding waves. Each rapid rise and launch over a crest was a delight, yet tempered with my unshakable feeling of anxiety.

We both turned to surf, paddling rapidly to catch a wave. I rode one steep wall as it collided with the next, almost doubling in height. The focus of the wave shifted, and I whipped my craft around from its left diagonal into a right in order to remain with the peak and dropped into the hole that was yawning beneath me. At this point another peak shifted into synchronization, abruptly adding to the steepness of the wave I was on and causing it to explode into spray. My kayak plunged, tripped end over end, and was buried by the falling water.

My anxiety turned immediately to panic. I went for a roll too quickly and botched it, trying to roll against the stream. I tried again and ended sculling for a moment as my kayak lurched up the steep face of the next erratic wave. I sank under once more.

My third attempt was successful, but my sprayskirt was off. Wobbling wildly, I fumbled at it and managed to flick it back into position as the sea around me pitched and leaped. I had water in my kayak and was struggling to stay upright. I lurched through the waves toward the shore aiming across the stream.

Ray spotted me and looked questioningly. I headed toward the rocks, and Ray helped me with a landing beneath the cliff. Even now I felt clumsy. Whether my feelings of uneasiness made me perform badly that day or whether I was less adept that day but able to sense it, I'm not really sure.

Some days your intuition tells you that something is not quite right. Sometimes it pays to listen to those feelings. If you're in doubt, listen to your doubts. There's no shame in bowing out and waiting for another day. This wasn't the only day I've felt uncertain about what I was planning to do. Now, at last, I'm learning to be more in touch with that intuition.

The Learning Process

You can learn from watching others, from watching surfing videos, from having maneuvers explained, from studying books, or by getting out there and learning by experience. The best way is to have a good teacher who will apply different methods to make your learning as easy as possible. We all, however, experience some basic learning steps.

When we first learn a skill, we need a lot of concentration to handle what we are doing, and we are less aware of other things going on around us. If we look around us, we have to pause in what we are doing. Practice makes the move we are learning automatic. When we no longer need to think about the move, we can concentrate on what's going on around us. Practice makes our reaction time quicker, and the linked strokes we use to complete a move become a familiar pathway to follow.

Begin slowly. Learn the correct basic kayak-handling skills first; then when they become automatic, apply them to small waves. Small waves are slower than big ones, giving you more time to respond to what happens. That's why I recommend playing in the soup to begin with, limiting your practice to waist-deep water. Once you have mastered the sideways slide, a diagonal run, and a zigzag, you may be ready to venture on to green waves.

Some of the more advanced moves require larger waves because speed is simply insufficient to carry out those maneuvers on small waves. A 360 spin on a green wave, for example, requires a steep slope, and it just won't happen on a tiny wave: You need to have the skill to maneuver your kayak into the right position on a sufficiently large wave before you can attempt the move. Build up your surfing skill gradually until you are unafraid of attempting new moves in such situations.

As you progress, your confidence will increase with your success. Even so it may take only one long swim to knock the confidence out of you. If you feel scared to go back out, I can assure you this feeling is normal and nothing to be ashamed of. It may take time to regain your former confidence, but the best way to do so is to move back into smaller waves and practice your skills there. When you are ready to tackle something just a bit larger, you will know you're ready. In the meantime resist

If it seems you are heading for the washing machine, take a deep breath and relax!

Regain control when you return to the surface.

any peer pressure to head out into the bigger stuff. Remember, it's normal for this "recovery" time to be quite lengthy. Accept that, and get on with enjoying smaller waves for a while in the knowledge that this is just part of the learning cycle. It happens to pretty much everybody.

When you get "trashed," what do you think about? The more you can relax, the easier it becomes to stick it out. Obviously you still need to physically grip into your kayak and cling to your paddle. It's your mind you need to relax. Your kayak may feel as though it's cartwheeling out of control somewhere way underwater in a frenzy of foam. Probably it is. But sooner or later the break will lose its power and offer you the opportunity to roll back up. Relax and wait. Bailing out seldom puts you in a better position, and if it does, that's only temporary. "Hanging in there" is a state of mind that you can work toward in wee increments. Practice by deliberately waiting upside down while small waves pass you. Build up to more turbulent situations. Some paddlers are more confident upside down than others and can immediately feel relaxed under there, whereas others take a long time to build that confidence. Whichever category you fall into, it's something worth working on.

When you progress to the more complex moves, it may be hard to find suitable waves that will let you go out and repeatedly perform the same maneuver in the same way. Surfing is a reactive sport. You need to respond to the way a wave breaks rather than superimposing a sequence of maneuvers that you have decided on beforehand. It's like driving a car around town: You may have a route planned, but you have to respond to the flow of traffic, parked cars, and pedestrians and you must regulate your speed and route accordingly. Your surfing run should be improvised, composed from a series of little rehearsed pieces strung together in the mood of the moment at the appropriate speed and in the most appropriate sequence.

Feeling Relaxed

As you progress, try to take more time during the moves you make on the wave. Slow down your paddle movements and concentrate on your edging. Relax your grip on your paddle and make every change of paddle position deliberate. This doesn't necessarily make your turns slower but does seem to

Relax! Most of your control is through edging.

give you more time to think during the same turns. You use less energy to attain the same results.

Shipping Gear

Trying new surfing locations can be exciting and refreshing and can encourage you to adapt and develop new skills. I learned to surf in the heavy, irregular waves of the English Channel, fighting the dumping shore break to launch from steep shingle beaches. My whole outlook on surfing changed when I first experienced the crisp green faces of Atlantic swells in Cornwall. But when you travel, you can seldom find a place that will rent you a kayak for surfing. Often your best alternative is to carry your own kayak with you.

Cartopping

A good roof rack can be expensive, but generally you get what you pay for. There is a rack designed specially to fit almost every car, and some manufacturers offer attachments that enable you to adapt their standard system to almost any car. Look for a sturdy rack, and invest in a locking system to lock it into position—I'll never forget the time I reached the shore to find the roof rack missing from the car.

Cradles and upright bars are accessories to your racks that will hold your kayak more firmly in position. Cradles give a shaped support for either your upright kayak or your inverted one. As an alternative upright bars enable you to secure

Car-topping: Tie your load securely.

your kayak on edge, where it will hold less rainwater, and to carry several kayaks stacked against one another. Bear in mind that sand will scratch. To minimize scratching, try to remove as much sand as possible before strapping kayaks against one another, and to minimize scratching on the decks, load them hull to hull. Use nylon webbing straps designed for securing loads, or strong line, to secure your kayak. An extra line from bow and stern to the front and rear fenders of your car will safeguard against your kayak's leaving your car should your roof rack fail or a collision occur.

A locked rack also gives you something to cable your kayak to for security. Use a plastic-sleeved, stainless-steel cable to thread around your seat or through a specially fitted security loop, and then loop it around your roof rack before locking with a padlock.

If you do carry your kayak upright, you can prevent it from filling with rainwater by using a cockpit cover. This item is similar to a sprayskirt but without the tube for your waist, although it may cause you difficulty cabling the kayak for security. Generally the amount of water a kayak will hold when carried on its side is minimal.

Flying

All the airlines I questioned will allow you to carry your kayak as checked luggage on your flight. Most, however, do not have the category *kayak* or *surf kayak* defined as such. More frequently baggage checkers will have the word *surf board* or *paddle board* on their list and will be able to use that to charge you appropriately. Any item not specifically on their list may be a problem for them to categorize, however. The words *kayak* and *surf kayak* seldom appear on these lists, and a standard way to categorize an unlisted item is to charge you the maximum listed rate for excess baggage.

You will find it easier and cheaper to check in your "paddle board" (it's a kind of surfboard) if you have it packaged like a piece of baggage. Companies such as Salamander have specially tailored carrybags designed to take surf kayaks and larger ones to take whitewater kayaks. They are fitted with carrying handles and windows for destination address tickets, and so they make life easy for the baggage handler. Though this is no guarantee for the safe handling of your kayak, you do stand a better chance of having your kayak handled well in transit. Cardboard and bubble-wrap packaging by itself will not make carrying easy for the baggage handler and will make it harder for you to convince the check-in staff that this is standard check-in baggage. Still, I would be wary of transporting a prized fiberglass or carbon-fiber composite kayak in this way. I would be more confident with plastic!

The length of your kayak may prevent you from flying with it on certain aircraft. The loading doors of some aircraft are too small for baggage longer than 9 feet, and some smaller planes cannot even take that. The weight limit per item of baggage is usually around seventy pounds. A plastic whitewater or surf kayak generally weighs between thirty and forty pounds. Depending on the weight of your kayak in its bag, you may be able to stow all your gear inside and still weigh in at below the limit. But take note: Wet gear will weigh a lot more than dry. Thus dry everything before your return journey or you may find yourself paying a substantial excess-weight charge for the privilege of carrying some salt water home.

Prices vary with the airline. Of the airlines I questioned, one allowed a "surfboard" to go free of extra charge as one of a maximum of two pieces of

A Salamander kayak bag and the blue protective bag for the take-apart paddle simplify travel by public transport, whether by air, rail, or ferry.

checked baggage. There was no size limit, providing the board was well wrapped and would fit on the plane used for that flight. By contrast most other airlines quoted a $50 to $70 surcharge, and one quoted $120. But bear in mind that airlines differ in their passenger fares too, so shop around for the best overall cost of flight plus surcharge.

Finally, figure out how you will get from your destination airport to the beach of your choice. If you intend to hire a rental car, it will almost certainly not have a roof rack. I suggest you take foam cradles (available at kayak stores) to protect the roof and secure your kayak, together with lines to secure the ends of your kayak to the car fenders. Tie off the center of each line to an end grab on the kayak, then spread each end as wide as possible to secure it to the fender to make the load stable.

Rail

Where rail services exist, it's normally easy to transport your kayak in the same way that you can a bicycle, although you will have to leave it in a special freight car, not provided on every service. The charge on a trip such as one from Seattle to San Francisco at the time of this writing was $5.00, compared with the $50.00 minimum quoted by air for the same route. But do check in advance what maximum length an item can be. Some "guard's vans" on British trains are too short for whitewater kayaks.

Freight (Air, Land, or Sea)

It's possible to freight your kayak overland using standard carriers, provided the craft is suitably packaged, but you will need a delivery address and will need to plan ahead to send the kayak in advance. Land freight within the United States can take six to ten days from the Northwest to the Southeast. Likewise if you intend to travel overseas to surf, you could ship your kayak, but it is time-consuming; transatlantic shipping takes some fourteen to nineteen days plus delays at either end. Air freight can be quicker, but neither method can normally provide you with a reliable date on which you can begin surfing. My recommendation for a long journey? Take your kayak with you by plane.

TRANSPORT MANEUVERS

Once in order to paddle a river in Arctic Canada, we strapped two kayaks at a time beneath the fuselage of a four-seater plane and made several trips to get us and our gear to the starting point. On another occasion we cut two sea kayaks in half to fly them on a scheduled flight to Canada from the United Kingdom, when the only service available had a 10-foot-long maximum length for any item. We joined the pieces together again on arrival. At Port St. Louis, on arriving at the Mediterranean after a Trans-France kayaking trip through the canal and river system, two of us hitchhiked with our 20-foot-long double kayak to the Marseilles railway station, getting a ride with a woman in a Citroën 2 CV. From Marseilles the kayak traveled as accompanied luggage on the train, for which there was an additional but not exorbitant charge. If you truly want to get somewhere different with your kayak, there is almost certainly a way to do so.

Appendixes

Appendix A
Selected Surfing Locations

My companion Geoff and I were making our way north up the western coast of Iceland during a circumnavigation of the island when we came across a sandbank across which lines of perfectly formed waves were peeling in crystal-clear water. There was no alternative but to stop and surf.

Loaded sea kayaks designed for straight tracking can be surprisingly agile on waves. We carved across the faces like a couple of schoolkids on a trackway of ice, following each other in turn to zip diagonally toward the deeper water and to cruise out onto the calmness without getting caught by the break. Sheer nectar! But then Geoff caught one a little late, and in his eagerness to avoid getting a soaking he capsized. When he rolled up, it was obvious that he had the "head between two bricks" feeling from the icy water. We left our perfect surf spot and continued north.

Cold it may be, but there are many excellent surfing places around Iceland and nobody out there surfing them!

In this appendix I highlight several notable surfing areas and beaches. These are intended as samples only, for the possibilities are endless. I hesitate to pinpoint the exact location of certain excellent surf breaks because of the limited size of the location and the probable effect of an increase in surfers there. Likewise there are so many surf locations worldwide that I cannot do more than sow a few seeds of ideas here for surfing in just a couple of countries. Below I draw your attention to areas where there are clusters of good beaches, locations where beaches are long, and places where surf competitions have been held. Use my suggestions as a starting point for research and exploration and you too will discover some gems.

For some of the areas outlined, swell reports are

available. For details consult the phone book and check local newspapers. Some television weather reports also indicate the state of the sea. If you are traveling to a new area, try to locate local kayak and surfing clubs, and discover where the nearest outdoor activity centers, outfitters, and surf shops are; these can be valuable sources of local information. New areas sometimes present hazards you may not have encountered before—perhaps deadly jellyfish (in places like Australia), weaver fish, or strong alongshore currents. The more local information you can discover, the better.

Surfing in the United States

Washington State

The breakwater at Westport provides suitable conditions in most weather. Outside, or south of the breakwater, offers the most reliable Pacific surf on a gently shelving sand beach. Inside, or north of the breakwater, refraction produces perfectly shaped swells that break onto a number of smaller beaches. These are typically surfable when the waves are stormblown and ragged outside the breakwater, but otherwise expect much smaller waves here.

La Push to the north is the traditional venue of the West Coast surf frolic each year that takes advantage of the January storm surf. At other times of the year, the chance of smaller but well-formed waves is greater here. This beach is piled with driftwood trees along the high-tide line—a typical feature of many of the beaches in this area.

Makah Beach is on the Pacific coast just south from Cape Flattery at the northwest point of Washington State. Cross the peninsula from Neah Bay, taking a left turn across the river and a right to take you south along the coast. There is a put-in on your right. The surf is frequently smaller close to the river mouth at the north end of the bay and larger in the middle of the bay.

Oregon

For gently breaking surf suitable for learning, try Pacific City Beach. Here the shore shelves gradually, and so it is possible to stand up even at some distance from the shore. Waves break far out and re-form and break several times on their way to shore, diminishing in power with every break.

Northern California

Drive the Northern California coast and you'll pass many sandy beaches with surf. Though it seems almost pointless to single out individual breaks, do try Half Moon Bay, south of San Francisco's Golden Gate Bridge. This is the home of the Tsunami Rangers, a thrill-seeking bunch of kayakers. Just to the north is the notorious Maverick reef break; walk the headland to watch it in heavy weather.

Santa Cruz, a little to the south, is a venue for surfing competitions and a lively mecca for board surfers.

Try also Monterey Bay, to the south. I have watched dolphins surf the waves here, and as a contrast to your surfing explore the coast from the town to watch sea lions sunbathe and sea otters feed in the kelp beds.

Southern California

Ventura and Faria Beach, just north of Ventura, are good bets. For local information contact Paddlesports in Santa Barbara or Patagonia in Ventura. Malibu, a familiar name to surfers, tends to be crowded and competitive. County Line (between Los Angeles and Ventura) is also busy, but there's a great fruit stand off the beach if competition is too fierce. In Los Angeles try Newport Beach, Huntington Beach, or Laguna Beach.

North Carolina

Hatteras, on the Outer Banks, is a good surfing area. Likewise, Sunset Beach has gentle breakers and is not too crowded. Paulis Island has a good point break at the south end.

South Carolina

Folly Beach, just south of Charleston, presents a long stretch of sand beach, and a drive along the coast road here will reveal the best spots. For added interest watch out for dolphins and sea turtles—I've see both when I have surfed here. Myrtle Beach and Surfside are good beaches for learning with mostly gentle breakers.

Florida

Sebastian inlet, the jetties at Fort Pierce, Cocoa Beach and the Canaveral seashore, and the New Smyrna Beach are all popular destinations. Much of the Florida Atlantic coast north of Vero Beach can collect good swell, so advice here is to scout the beach from route A1A to find a good spot with a good break, easy coastal access, and not too many surfers.

The jetties at Venice on the Gulf Coast extend west to the north and south of the Venice Pass, south of Casey Key. Park on Casey Key at Nokomis Beach to access the northwest-facing beach, or park south of the jetties to access the southwest-facing beach.

Hawaii

Maui: Surfing is best on the south shore in summer and the north shore in winter. When conditions are too big for your comfort, try the opposite shore. Winter storms make the surf bigger in this season. South shore beaches include Thousand Peaks, Lasiopoko (a gentle break that's good for beginners), and Dumps (not a reference to dumping waves but the dump that used to be nearby). North shore beaches include Hookipi and Jaws, where surfers are towed onto the wave to reach sufficient speed to catch the wave. Surfers at Jaws ride waves from 20 to 40 feet high.

Oahu: This is the location of many classic board surfing beaches, such as Sunset, Pipeline, and Waimea. These are all north shore beaches. Ala Moana and Waikiki are south shore beaches suitable for beginners. Many people also kayak at Kailua (north and west).

Surfing in the United Kingdom

England

Devon and Cornwall

Devon and Cornwall offer some of the finest surfing beaches in the United Kingdom, with the most reliable surf. The two English counties cover the end of the peninsula, which extends to the southwest of England into the Atlantic Ocean. The region is of a rocky character, and cliffs border many fine sandy bays, with beaches in the area that face in almost every direction. As a result it is almost always possible to find a clean break somewhere, no matter from which direction the wind blows, and there is almost always somewhere sheltered to surf on small waves when the swell is big. In short you will find a lot of variety and a lot of choice. Historically popular surf areas in Cornwall are Bude, where many national surf kayaking competitions have been held, and Newquay, with its multifaceted coast. Farther south, to the north and south coasts respectively of the Penwith Peninsula near Land's End, are the towns of St. Ives and Penzance. A short drive across the peninsula from one to the other offers a good alternative, depending on the weather and swell direction. In Devon a favored spot is Woolacombe.

If you are a seasoned surfer seeking the largest waves in the area, go to Cornwall. Bypass St. Ives and Penzance and continue to Land's End. Immediately north of Land's End itself, by the village of Sennen, lies Sennen Cove, with its sheltered harbor to the south and the more exposed Gwenver Beach to the north of the bay. Beware of the undertow here. Generally if the surf is moderate elsewhere in Cornwall, it will be big here.

South Coast

Not far from the "nodding donkey" oil pumps on the cliff at Kimmeridge is a fine break over ledges of oil-rich shale. Scout this one out before committing yourself. Examination of the map also indicates a long beach called Chesil Beach a little farther east. This is a steep shingle bank that offers little but a heavy shore break. Don't be misled.

On the Isle of Wight southeast from the famous chalk stacks, the Needles, lies Freshwater Bay. This catches uninterrupted swells as they pass up the English Channel from the southwest. The surf can be great when there is a depression to the southwest of Britain, but watch for the shore break, and be warned that the tide runs swiftly past the Needles should you be tempted to paddle around to see them.

Just to the east of the Isle of Wight lies West Wittering. West Wittering can offer well-shaped surf, but like many other southeastern beaches it has breakwaters segmenting the shore and at high tide dumpers onto shingle can occur.

For surf kayakers in London and the southeast of England, Camber Sands in Rye Bay offers probably the closest and easiest access to surf. Here you occasionally experience swell, but more often windblown waves. Access to a long sandy beach is easy. Most of the rest of the south coast of England east of the Isle of Wight is made up

of steep beaches of rounded flints that produce dumping waves at high tide but may offer ridable waves toward low tide. It's not an area I'd travel to for surf unless I were in the region. Don't expect waves without wind.

East Coast

The east coast of England is not especially noted for its fine surf, but you can find good waves on sand beaches at locations such as South Shields.

Wales

The Gower Peninsula in South Wales is a small place with a number of interesting surf locations. Expect the area to be busy in the tourist season but off-season look around for both beach and reef breaks.

Pembrokeshire, in the region around St. Davids and in St. Brides Bay, catches southwesterly swell. It has a number of good, sizable beaches, such as Whitesands Bay, but scout around and you'll find plenty of alternatives here. If you are a skilled wave rider with a whitewater background, seek local paddlers in St. Davids who can tell you more about the "Bitches," a tidal rapid beside the island of Ramsey that produces ridable standing waves at certain periods of the tidal cycle. To surf here, you will need to cross the fiercely tidal Ramsey Sound, and because there are landing restrictions on the island of Ramsey, local knowledge is essential.

In North Wales the long beach of Hells Mouth or Porth Neigwl is perfectly positioned near the extremity of the Lleyn Peninsula to catch southwesterly swell moving up the Irish Sea from the Atlantic. Storms centered in the vicinity of the Azores spawn the best waves to arrive here. Farther north on the island of Anglesey, Newborough Beach will collect similar swell, but the bay has more sandbanks and the waves are generally smaller and less regular. You'll find many smaller beaches farther north on Anglesey, but windblown waves rather than swell tend to predominate here.

Scotland

Scotland boasts many beautiful locations for surfing, but some of the best are fairly inaccessible white shell-sand beaches along the western shores of the Outer Hebrides. Notable also is the bay at Thurso, which can produce an excellent reef break, the site of international surf-kayaking competitions.

Appendix B
The Beaufort Wind Scale

Wind speed is traditionally measured from the bridge of a ship, around 30 feet from the surface, not at kayaker level, where you will generally experience less wind than at 30 feet. Wind speed, in conjunction with the direction and dura-tion of the wind and with the fetch, enables us to forecast the nature of storm surf and predict swell. If you travel to different countries to surf, you will hear this wind speed expressed in miles per hour, in knots, in kilometers per hour, in meters per second, or as a number on the Beaufort Wind Scale. On the following page I have drawn up a comparative table so that you can convert the information in a local forecast into something you can relate to.

BEAUFORT WIND SCALE

FORCE	KNOTS	MILES PER HOUR	KILOMETERS PER HOUR	METERS PER SECOND
0	1 or less	1 or less	1.6 or less	0.5 or less
1	1–3	1–3	1.6–6	0.5–2
2	4–6	5–7	6–12	2–3
3	7–10	8–11	13–19	3–5
4	11–16	13–18	20–30	5–8
5	17–21	19–24	31–39	8–10
6	22–27	25–31	40–50	11–14
7	28–33	32–38	51–61	14–17
8	34–40	39–46	62–74	17–20
9	41–47	47–54	75–87	20–24
10	48–55	55–63	88–102	24–28
11	55–65	64–75	103–120	29–33
12	66 or more	76 or more	121 or more	33 or more

Beaufort Wind Force	Description	Sea Condition	Sea State
1	Calm	Like mirror	Smooth
2	Light air	Ripples like scales	Calm
3	Light breeze	Small wavelets, glassy crests, not breaking	Calm
4	Moderate breeze	Small waves, becoming longer, fairly frequent white horses	Slight
5	Fresh breeze	Moderate waves, more pronounced long form, many white horses, possibly some spray	Moderate
6	Strong breeze	Large waves begin to form, white crests more extensive everywhere, probably some spray	Rather rough
7	Near gale	Sea heaps up with white foam from breaking waves	Rather rough
8	Gale	Moderately high waves of greater length, much foam	Rough
9	Strong gale	High waves, dense streaks of foam along the direction of the wind	Very rough
10	Storm		

Glossary

A lot of sports have their own vocabulary, and surf kayaking is one of those sports. Apart from numerous technical terms to puzzle over, local expressions often come and go like the surf itself. The local language you'll have to pick up yourself, but some of the internationally accepted words and technical terms are defined here.

Backwash

The water from the previous wave flowing back down the shore to meet the next oncoming wave.

Beaufort wind scale

A measure of wind speed. See Appendix B.

Bore

Tidal wave that typically runs inland as a result of the funneling effect on a fast-rising tide into an estuary.

Bottom turn

A turn in which the kayak is surfed out into the trough ahead of the breaking wave, then back onto the face.

Bouncer

A radical turn in which the kayak is surfed along the face toward the break, then edged to bounce the hull against the breaking edge of the wave through the turn.

Bow

The front end of your kayak.

Brace

Stabilizing position for you when your balance is maintained with the aid of your paddle.

Breaker

A breaking wave.

Broach

Typically the effect of the wind on a boat under way that turns it up into the wind. In surfing the term is commonly used for an instance in which a kayak is turned broadside by the effect of a wave.

Buddy

Term commonly used to describe a surfing partner who keeps watch while you surf and vice versa.

"C to C"

Either a type of roll or the body movement used in a braced recovery or roll whereby the body is arched sideways in one direction to begin and in the other to finish.

Capillary waves

The fine surface waves that run with gusts of wind, traveling at the same speed as the wind.

Catch

The point at which your blade is planted in the water ready to begin a stroke.

Celerity

The speed a wave moves through the water.

Closing out

The simultaneous collapse of a long section of wave.

Convergence

The compression of a wave, which increases its size, caused by refraction of the wave around a point or shoal. From above the wave appears to wrap around the shoal.

Crest

The sharp top edge of the wave just before or as the wave breaks.

Cutback

A turn toward the break from a diagonal run, followed by a return to the original direction of surfing once the kayak has been positioned where the wave is steeper, closer to the break.

Deepwater wave

A wave that has not "felt the bottom." Swells begin to change shape when the depth of water beneath the trough is less than half the wavelength—a phenomenon called *feeling the bottom*.

Depression

A weather term referring to an area of low pressure around which the wind blows in a counterclockwise direction in the Northern Hemisphere and a clockwise direction in the Southern Hemisphere.

Diagonal run

A surfing run angled somewhere in the region of forty-five degrees from the direction of the wave, where the course is usually maintained only by a downwave braced paddle blade, with the kayak edged into the wave. Removal of the paddle from the water on a diagonal run will result in a broach.

Divergence

The lengthening or stretching of a swell that causes it to weaken and diminish in size, a result of refraction.

Diver's ring

A plastic hoop that, slipped inside a latex neck seal of a drysuit, holds the seal open.

Dropping in

Catching a wave that is already being ridden by another surfer.

Drybag

A resealable storage sack designed to keep items dry, as in a kayak.

Drysuit

A complete waterproof bodysuit sealed at the ankles (or feet), wrists, and neck with latex seals to keep out water. A *drytop* is a waterproof jacket that has wrist and neck seals.

Dumper

A wave that breaks abruptly as a result of reaching a steeply shelving bottom.

Duration

The time a wind has been blowing over the sea from a single direction. A strong wind will take a long time to build up the maximum wave height for that wind speed. It may take two days of gale-force winds before the waves reach the maximum height for that wind force.

Edging

Holding one side (rail, or edge) of the kayak down in the water by positioning body weight on that side.

Ender

An end-over-end or half-somersault move performed in a kayak in the surf.

End grab

A rope loop, toggle, line, or handle at the bow or stern of your kayak.

Exposure bag

A large bag about 3-by-6 feet to 4-by-8 feet in size, generally made of heavy-duty polyethylene or proofed nylon and used for emergency treatment of hypothermia or for sitting inside to escape the chill of the wind.

Fetch

The distance over which the wind may blow. Gale-force winds cannot produce large waves in a small pond, but they can do so on the ocean, where the fetch is greater.

Foot pump

A foot-operated pump used to keep the inside of a kayak dry.

Green room

The inside of a tube formed by the crest of a breaker pitching out toward the trough. When surfing inside the tube, the paddler is known to be "in the green room."

Green wave

Unbroken ridable wave face.

Group survival tent

A squat baglike tent in which a group can crouch or sit for shelter.

Gunwale

The outside perimeter of the kayak, where the deck joins the hull.

Height

Vertical distance from the trough to the crest.

Hip flick

The sharp upward shift of one hip toward the head, which is simultaneously brought down.

Lapstrap

The webbing strap with quick release used to hold a wave-ski rider to his or her ski. Used in conjunction with footstraps, the lapstrap enables the rider to remain in his or her seat when inverted and also to roll.

Lieback

A body movement sometimes used during a roll in which you arch your back around your rear deck.

Lull

The period of smaller wave activity between sets of larger waves.

Neoprene

A synthetic rubber insulating material used for the production of wetsuits. The material used for surf kayaking wetsuits is typically between 2 and 4 millimeters thick and filled with tiny bubbles, which provide the insulation.

Offside

The side of your kayak opposite to that on which you are using your paddle.

Onside

The side of your kayak on which you are using your paddle.

Overfalls

Tidal rapids in which a strong tidal stream is restricted in depth, causing a speeding up of the stream.

Paddle leash

A length of line or bungee attaching the paddle to the wrist of a kayaker.

Pawlata roll

An extended paddle sculling roll named after H. W. Pawlata, the Austrian credited with using this particular Inuit technique to become the first European to perform a kayak roll.

Pearl

The term used when the bow of a surfing kayak buries in the water at the base of a wave.

Period

The time it takes for a complete trough and crest to pass a particular spot—for example, the time from crest to crest.

Personal Flotation Device (PFD)

The American name for the waistcoast- or vest-shaped buoyancy aid worn by kayakers and other boaters.

Pirouette

A lateral spin performed when the kayak is on end in the surf.

Pocket

The steep face of the wave immediately adjacent to the break.

Point break

A break where waves are refracted around a headland and peel constantly away from the inside shore of the headland. Point breaks can give some of the longest rides.

Popout

An occurrence in which a kayak leaves the water on end as a result of water pressure on the submerged end during an ender in which the kayak has penetrated the water to a greater depth than usual.

Power face

The face of the paddle blade used to grip the water when forward paddling. It is the concave face of a curved blade.

Put-across roll

A roll in which the paddle is held perpendicular to the kayak on the surface to provide a high brace with which the kayak is righted.

Rail

The outer edge of the kayak, which is held down in the wave when surfing to aid tracking and turning.

Reef break

A break over a shoal or ledge.

Refraction

The change of direction a swell takes when it feels bottom. Typically the wave will bend around toward a shore as soon as it feels bottom.

Rip

The riverlike current flowing out to sea from a beach as a result of the soup being carried onshore. The rip may also flow along the shore to join the main outflow. A rip is sometimes known as a *runout*.

Roll

The righting of an inverted kayak, usually achieved with the aid of the paddle against the water and a simultaneous sideways body movement.

Roller coaster

A repeated rise and fall on the wave face, performed while surfing diagonally.

Rudder

In surfing terms a paddle position near the stern that steers the kayak, either with the back of the blade against the water in a low-brace position, which steers the kayak toward that blade, or in a high-brace power-face-against-the-water position, which steers the kayak away from that paddle blade.

Runout

See *Rip*.

Screw roll

A sculling roll with the paddle held in a normal grip (that is, not extended by moving the hands toward one end of the shaft) sculled from bow to stern.

Sculling

The constant to-and-fro planing movement of the horizontal paddle blade across the surface of the water in such a way as to maintain lift, or with a vertical paddle in such a way as to provide a lateral pull. For rolling it is usual to scull across the surface.

Sea

The chaotic wave effect whereby wind in a weather system is generating waves that interact from several directions.

Set

A series of larger swells arriving at a beach one after another as a group.

Setup

The position of your body and paddle underwater when you are ready to begin a roll.

Shallow-water waves

Waves that have "felt the bottom" and are in a depth of water of less than half the wavelength.

Shoal

A shallow patch surrounded by deeper water. Swells peak over shoals, and typically a wave will wrap around a shoal, causing a horseshoe-shaped break.

Soup

The tumbling white part of a breaking wave. The soup actually surfs shoreward on the face of the wave.

Spectrum (wave spectrum)

A measure that, because not all waves on a given day travel at the same rate, gives the range of time from the slowest to the fastest—for example, from three to twenty seconds.

Spotter

A person who watches out for the safety of surfers from a vantage point typically on the beach.

Sprayskirt

The removable fabric cover that spans the gap between the deck of the kayak and the seated paddler, keeping water from the cockpit.

Stern

The back end of a kayak.

Styr roll

A roll using an extended paddle (a hand grip shifted toward one end of the shaft) in which the blade is sculled from stern to bow (as opposed to the Pawlata, which uses a bow-to-stern scull).

Swash

The water that rises up the beach on the arrival of a wave on the shore. This water will return down the beach as backwash.

Sweep

The turning stroke whereby the blade describes a semicircle from bow to stern (forward sweep) or stern to bow (reverse sweep) relative to the position of the kayak. Actually the blade remains almost stationary while the kayak turns.

Swell waves

Waves that have moved away from the winds generating them. Swell generally has a period of ten seconds or more.

Tidal bore

A wave or series of waves behind which the water level is higher than the water level in front.

Tidal race

A tidal rapid caused by a constricted tidal flow. Waves formed by the current move against the direction of flow, as on a river rapid.

Transit points

Two fixed objects that when lined up, one more distant than the other, can be used to detect drift across the water.

Tube

A tunnel momentarily formed when the crest of a wave pitches forward to enclose a ridable face.

Undertow

A current of water that runs along the seabed from the shore, frequently associated with a heavy dumping shore break. The water escapes by flowing beneath the surface, rather than as a rip, which is more commonly associated with a surf break.

Wavelength

The distance between one crest and the next.

Wave ski

Essentially a sit-on-top, paddle-powered surfboard.

Wetsuit

A figure-hugging, heat-insulating neoprene suit designed to trap a thin layer of water (which becomes warmed by body heat) against the skin.

Wind speed

A measure used to forecast storm surf and predict swell. Wind speed is expressed in miles per hour, in knots, in kilometers per hour, in meters per second, or as a number on the Beaufort Wind Scale. See Appendix B.

Wind waves

Waves being formed by the wind at a given time. Generally chaotic and irregular, wind waves create a "sea" and normally have a period of less than eight seconds.

Zigzag

A series of alternating turns that result in the kayak surfing a zigzag course along a straight line toward shore.

Index

About the Author

Nigel Foster has been surf kayaking almost as long as he's been sea kayaking—nearly thirty years. He holds the highest level of British Canoe Union Coach award in sea kayaking and surf kayaking and the Senior Instructor and advanced proficiency award in whitewater kayaking. He was one of a select group of British Canoe Union coaches responsible for establishing the surf coaching program now operated by the BCU.

Nigel is a regular contributor to *Sea Kayaker* magazine and is the author of *Nigel Foster's Sea Kayaking,* second edition (1997, Globe Pequot and Fernhurst [U.K.]); *Canoeing: A Beginner's Guide to the Kayak* (1990, Fernhurst); and *Open Canoe Technique* (1996, Fernhurst). Through his classes, lectures, and other work he is internationally recognized as a sea kayaking authority.

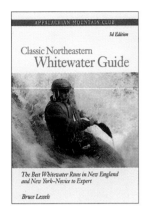  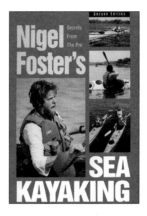 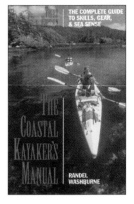